Sensuous Glory

To David
with many thanks
& every blessing

About the authors

Donald [A. M.] Allchin is Honorary Professor in the University of Wales in Bangor and has written extensively in the fields of theology and contemporary spirituality. His publications include *Resurrection's Children*, *The Joy of All Creation – an Anglican Meditation on the Place of Mary*, *Praise Above All*, and *God's Presence Makes the World*.

D. Densil Morgan is Senior Lecturer in the School of Theology and Religious Studies, University of Wales, Bangor. He is an ordained Baptist minister and author of works on Christmas Evans and Karl Barth. His latest volume, *The Span of the Cross: Christian Religion and Society in Wales, 1914–2000* has been recently published by the University of Wales Press. He is married with two children.

Patrick Thomas has been rector of the Carmarthenshire hill parishes of Brechfa, Abergorlech and Llanfihangel Rhos y Corn since 1984, and is director of post-ordination training in the Diocese of St David's. He is an honorary member of the Gorsedd of Bards and a former member of the Welsh Language Board, and has published books and articles in both English and Welsh.

SENSUOUS GLORY

The Poetic Vision of D. Gwenallt Jones

Donald Allchin
and
D. Densil Morgan

with translations by
Patrick Thomas

Foreword by
the Archbishop of Wales

CANTERBURY
PRESS
Norwich

First published in 2000 by The Canterbury Press Norwich
(a publishing imprint of Hymns Ancient & Modern Limited
a registered charity)
St Mary's Works, St Mary's Plain
Norwich, Norfolk, NR3 3BH
in partnership with The Centre for the Advanced Study of
Religion in Wales, University of Bangor

Translations of the poems by D. Gwenallt Jones
are by kind permission of the Gomer Press

British Library Cataloguing in Publication Data

A catalogue record for this book is available
from the British Library

ISBN 1-85311-349-2

Typeset by Rowland Phototypesetting,
Bury St Edmunds, Suffolk
Printed in Great Britain by
Biddles Ltd, Guildford and King's Lynn

Contents

Foreword
by the Archbishop of Wales

Some figures – T. S. Eliot, Thomas Merton – become voices for far more than their own individual experience; they encapsulate the struggles of a whole era, a whole class of people, and create a distinct imaginative world. For anyone who grew up in twentieth century Wales, Gwenallt has something of this character. His personal voice is matured in the context of an industrialism careless of life and welfare, first finding itself in the language of Marxist critique and then falling into the rhythm and cadence of a bleak but honest and impassioned Christianity, with its vision of humanity, reduced almost to animality (echoes of *King Lear*), scenting the redeeming blood from far off and howling with longing – one of Gwenallt's most outrageous and unforgettable images.

His growth towards a sacramental and Catholic perspective and his membership of the Anglican Church did not soften this vision, though it gave it far wider dimensions and a depth of underlying warmth and hope. When he abandoned Anglicanism, it could be seen in part as a protest in the name of the very catholicity he had learned in the Anglican Church, a protest against churchy intolerance and a bland indifference to the ways in which the gospel had woven itself into the culture and speech of *this* people and *this* place. For him, in the image of another familiar poem of his, 'Catholicity' was about the freedom of Christ and the gospel to translate themselves into the familiar landscape of everyday Welshness (or any other local identity) – the landscape inhabited by saints doing ordinary things in the light and grace of God – as in the great poem on St David.

In a late poem, not included here, part of a sequence on the Holy Land, he writes of the Church of All Nations at Gethsemane as a sign of how the churches are one only because of the agony and bloody sweat of the Garden, blood and sweat falling between

the Catholic rock:
the ecumenical garden:
the Evangelical olive tree.

It is another potent image of how tragedy and generosity are woven into his poetry in a way that gives it a rare spiritual authority. These penetrating essays and fine translations offer a whole theology in compressed form, a theology which in its mixture of harsh honesty and trans-figuring vision avoids sentimentality and vivifies tradition.

† Rowan Williams
March 2000

Preface

This book proceeds from a shared conviction of the importance of Gwenallt's work for the beginning of the twenty-first century, and from a sense that that importance is not sufficiently recognized today. Both the writers of the essays and the translator of the poems see, in this mid-twentieth century poet, a powerful and at times prophetic exponent of a catholic evangelicalism and an evangelical catholicism. This is an apprehension and experience of the Christian faith which we believe could have much to say to our contemporaries.

But while sharing a common conviction of the importance of our subject, the two essayists are vividly aware of the different ways in which they approach it. For one, who comes to Gwenallt, as to Wales, from afar (culturally, if not geographically, for Oxford is not all that far from the Welsh border), the poet was one of the first who helped him to understand something of the tradition and experience of the nation which lies so near to his own.

In his essay he has sought to convey something of the way in which Gwenallt may act as a guide for anyone who is seeking a closer and more realistic understanding of the things which go to make up the destiny and character of Wales. With his vivid and often striking images, with his love for what is particular and precise in his description of people and places, Gwenallt brings before us a memorable picture of the Wales of his time as he experienced it; a land of stark contrasts, with its ugliness and beauty, its glory and its shame.

In a remarkable way Gwenallt speaks of many aspects of the Welsh tradition, its industrial strand no less than its rural, its Methodist and post-Methodist inheritance no less than its medieval period. The writer seeks to place Gwenallt in a European and international perspective, convinced that it is in that context that he needs to be seen. Gwenallt, though rooted in his own time and place, has a remarkable sense of the unity of Europe and indeed of Christendom as a whole.

For the other writer, whose upbringing was in many ways so much closer to that of Gwenallt, the sense of identity with the subject he is dealing with is profound and urgent. For him, as a teenager, the work and example of Gwenallt was converting and life-giving. Thus he sets out the work of our writer, not from afar, but from very close at hand. He leads us through the successive phases of his work, to two of its final and finest statements, the poem to J. E. Daniel, the Bangor theologian, and the poem on the disaster of Aberfan.

In the course of his detailed discussion of Gwenallt's work, he does not ignore the challenge of the often negative assessments of Gwenallt's writing which have been made in Welsh criticism in the last two decades. But he argues that both from a literary and theological point of view there is much to be said on the other side. In particular in terms of their theology, he maintains that these poems show us in an incomparable fashion the way in which the universal may be expressed through the particular, the particular may embody and recapitulate the universal. Here is something vital to the inner development of twentieth-century Christianity, the recovery of a unity of vision which has given it the capacity to meet head-on some of the most inhuman manifestations of the destructive power of evil.

All his life Gwenallt had been confronted by the unacceptable manifestations of the capitalist system, its capitulation to human greed and its unconcern with human suffering. He had seen this in his father's death, he saw it again finally in the death of the children of Aberfan, in the silent tragedy of the village school. But more profoundly he saw his time as one in which apocalyptic powers of good and evil had been released into the world. There were evident powers of darkness and destruction at work in the Europe of the Holocaust and the concentration camps; but also present in the tumult there were unexpected powers of sacrificial goodness and love. These are things which altogether confound our customary measures of right and wrong. As Dietrich Bonhoeffer wrote, shortly before his execution in a Nazi prison, 'the villain and the saint have little to do with systematic ethical studies. They emerge from the primeval depths and by their appearance they tear open the infernal and the divine abyss from which they come, and enable us to see for a moment in to mysteries of which they had never dreamed.'

These mysteries, especially the paradoxical triumph of sacrificial love revealed in the deaths of the martyrs, perhaps the most powerful sign of the unity of Christians across their divisions, were matters on which Gwenallt pondered deeply. The catholic evangelicalism to which he had slowly won his way, far from being a piece of ecclesiastical joinery proved to be the source of a renewal of faith and experience which enabled him to see that deeper than the depths of human tragedy and loss are the depths of the redeeming love of God.

The two essays are followed by thirty-five poems by Gwenallt, newly translated by Patrick Thomas. These translations, with the notes that accompany them, make something of Gwenallt's vision accessible to readers who do not know Welsh, with the notes that accompany them, who are learning the language and who will be able to go to the originals and find in them the strength, the vividness and the directness which characterize so much of Gwenallt's writing.

Donald Allchin
D. Densil Morgan

PART ONE

Two Centenary Essays

Discovering a New World

DONALD ALLCHIN

I

The Factories and the Fields

Like most English people I grew up in almost total ignorance of the existence of Wales. Only in my thirties did I begin to discover that there was another people in the south of Britain with a language, a culture and a history of their own. While they were much less numerous than the English they certainly had inhabited this island which is both theirs and ours, considerably longer than we had.

There was quite a number of factors involved in the gradual opening of my eyes and ears to recognize the existence of this hitherto unknown world. One of the most important of them was the friendship of Herbert Hodges, at that time Professor of Philosophy in the University of Reading. He was a man who was no less English than I myself am, but one who had mastered the Welsh language in a very remarkable way. It was from the translations that he made, not for publication but for his own interest and for the pleasure of a few friends, that I first discovered the hymns of Ann Griffiths and Williams Pantycelyn. From him I also discovered the existence of a remarkable group of deeply committed Christian poets writing in the middle of the twentieth century. Four men in particular stood out,

Saunders Lewis, Waldo Williams, Euros Bowen and David Gwenallt Jones. Of these it was the last named who most impressed me at first reading. His verse came across powerfully even in translation; a verse which spoke directly of many of the deepest themes of Christian faith and of many of the most urgent needs of our mid-twentieth-century world.

With Gwenallt's help I found myself entering on a journey of discovery, the discovery of Wales, first the Nonconformist Wales of the years at the beginning of the last century, then the older world of a Wales whose Christian roots went back directly to the period when the Roman armies left Britain in 410. Gwenallt wrote much and on a great variety of subjects. He felt deeply responsible for the tradition of which he was a part. He longed to bring it alive in a new way in answer to the challenges of his own time. He longed to hand it on, not as a museum piece but as a living source of insight and understanding for the future.

I soon began to be acquainted with the outline of his life. He was born in 1899 in an industrial village in South Wales; a place called Pontardawe, not far north of Swansea. His father worked in the steel works there. In 1917 when he came to be called up, he registered as a conscientious objector. But as his objections to fighting in the war were more political than religious, his appeal was not accepted. He spent two years in prison in Wormwood Scrubs and Dartmoor, not the most pleasant of penal establishments.

Released from jail, he went to the University of Wales in Aberystwyth. There he discovered the profession which he was to follow for the rest of his days, that of a university teacher of the language and literature of Wales. There too he began to discover that he had a talent for writing verse. But it was only in the following decade that he began to publish his work, and only in 1939 did he produce his first substantial collection of poems. As he read and studied widely in these years so he began to find that the Christian faith, in which he had grown up and which he had abandoned in his adolescent discovery of socialism, was beginning to come back to him. Slowly, fitfully, he began to rediscover its contours. In 1944 he was confirmed as a member of the Church in Wales.

From 1939 until the time of his death in 1968 Gwenallt was recognized as one of the outstanding and most influential poets of his time in Welsh-speaking Wales. He was a poet whose outspoken expression of his Christian and political views attracted some and repelled others. He became known in a way which is difficult to imagine in the English-speaking world, where poets are hardly expected to be publicly recognized, controversial public figures.

Socially speaking, Gwenallt came from a solidly working-class, industrial background. Religiously his youth was shaped by the Nonconformity of his time, at that period at the height of its power and influence. His parents were actively committed members of the Calvinistic Methodist Church in Pontardawe, the body which represented most clearly the distinctive Methodist revival of eighteenth-century Wales. It was to this church that he returned towards the end of his life.

But Gwenallt's childhood was not only spent in the urban setting of Pontardawe. His parents had moved there only a few years before his birth and his holidays were regularly spent with older relatives, grandparents, aunts and uncles who were still following the rural way of life which his parents themselves had known as children, in the depths of Carmarthenshire. Gwenallt felt within himself the tension between the rural and the urban, the slow rhythm of life in the countryside before the mechanization of farming methods on the one side and the noise and busyness of the industrial world of South Wales before the First World War on the other. He tells us something of the impression which the chapel in the country made in his boyhood in his poem 'The Chapel in Carmarthenshire' (see *Translations*, no. 6 p. 103).

It is often asked whether the religion of Welsh Non-conformity was so strongly focused on the doctrine of redemption that it said little or nothing about the doctrine of creation. Certainly, if we look at the hymns we shall find a great emphasis laid on the sacrifice of the cross, on the mysterious transaction made on the hill of Calvary, on the death by which death is overcome. But the doctrine of God's creating and sustaining love is not absent from the hymns, nor was it from the preaching of the chapel, even if at times it was overshadowed by the message of redemption.

In this poem Gwenallt tells us something about the religion of the chapel in the countryside, as a lived and experienced reality which we should never have learnt from the texts of hymns and sermons taken by themselves. The chapel was indeed alive with the gospel, warm with the hymns of redemption, many of them written by poets who were near neighbours, whom everyone knew about. But outside there were the carriages which had brought the farmers to chapel, with their stamping horses, and all around the chapel were the fields ready for harvest. In practice, if not in theory, redemption and creation went together. The seasons of the agricultural year were the context in which the drama of salvation was played out and celebrated in hymns and preaching. It is striking that in what looks like a simple poem, descriptive of the chapel worship of an earlier period, the writer has brought together into one the two aspects of Christian faith and doctrine, God's work in creation, God's work in redemption, and shown their underlying unity. As we shall see, this is a recurrent theme in his work.

We may observe too that the poem was written at a time when Gwenallt was much influenced by the theology of Anglo-Catholicism. Certainly the chapel is furnished with the preaching of the gospel and the singing of the hymns; also it provides for its members at least one of the sacraments of the gospel, that is to say, baptism, and two of the sacramental rites of the Church, marriage and burial. But there is no mention here of the Supper of the Lord, the ordinance which we know was of deepest importance to Gwenallt himself. Its celebration depended, so he believed at this time, on a valid ministry, and according to the theology which he had accepted, that the chapel could not give. But even at this moment it is important to recognize what a positive picture he gives us of the worshipping life of the chapel. There is no repudiation of his earlier inheritance.

Of course the poem insists that God is worshipped not only in the countryside. His presence is no less real in the town even though it is there made known in very different circumstances. If in his poems Gwenallt writes much about the countryside, he writes more about the industrial villages in the south in which his childhood and adolescence were spent. Often what he says about them can be hard and bitter, sometimes almost despairing. In the years before the 1914 war he had already known fiercely fought strikes, as the workers struggled to gain more equitable conditions and better wages. In the 1920s his own father was killed in a hideous industrial accident, involving a fall of molten metal. In the 1930s there came the period of the Depression with its time of massive unemployment. Gwenallt saw much of the ugly face of capitalist society.

But I have chosen to represent Gwenallt's writing on this subject of the industrial south by a poem which shows us something of the human, hopeful side of this urban world; something which shows us the way in which Gwenallt sees God's presence at work in all things, not least in the society of the valleys: 'Pigeons' (*Translations*, no. 25 p. 134). In a brief but penetrating comment on this poem, Robert Rhys points to 'the image of the workers, released from their joyless, soul-destroying day job, by being restored and humanised by their interest in racing pigeons'. The pigeons form a link with the rural pre-industrial world, and with their element of sheer play, gratuity and freedom, they speak of genuinely human values and of the power of the Holy Spirit, 'the only regenerative agency that can transform and renew industrial society'.[1]

If Gwenallt was a man of his own time, he was also a man deeply conscious of earlier periods in history. The life and experience of the Christian community, of course, goes back far beyond the nineteenth century. It is rooted in Wales in what is called the Age of the Saints, the early centuries of Celtic Christianity in the period immediately following the fall of the Roman Empire. This earliest period was a time of disaster and destruction in which what seemed a firmly established civilization, suddenly crumbled and fell. Out of that death, the early Christians' faith in Christ crucified and risen brought unlooked-for new life and vision. In a major poem ('St David', *Translations*, no. 5 pp. 100–2) dedicated to the figure of St David, Gwenallt speaks of the saints as

> . . . our oldest ancestors
> Who built Wales on the foundation of
> The Cradle, the Cross and the Empty Grave.

He never forgets that early period which often seems strangely near in Wales, and which has never ceased to inspire and embolden the Church in subsequent ages.[2]

But there have been other moments of decisive significance in the Christian history of that country, not least the time towards the end of the sixteenth century when the Bible and the Book of Common Prayer were translated into Welsh. In 'Bishop William Morgan' (*Translations*, no. 11 pp. 112–13) we have a good example of a praise poem, one of the fundamental types of poetry in Welsh, a praise poem devoted to the man who had the most decisive part in the rooting of the Reformation in Wales, the translator of the Bible.

Each verse in this poem tells us something vital about the work of William Morgan and the little group of scholars who were involved with him in translating the Bible into Welsh. A language which has no official status in society and is not used for the administration of justice or the conduct of business is easily threatened with disintegration, with the possibility of falling into a group of disparate dialects. This is what happened both in Ireland and in Brittany. In Wales the fact that the Bible was translated and that it was used Sunday by Sunday in the worship of the great majority of the parish churches in Wales, meant that the standard, classical form of the language was not only established but became familiar in all parts of the country.

Without the translation of the Bible and the Book of Common Prayer in which it was enshrined, the laity of the Church, the great majority of whom were illiterate in the sixteenth and seventeenth centuries, would have remained totally disenfranchized. The services of the medieval Church had been in Latin, but they had been surrounded by a multitude of ceremonies and customs whose symbolism spoke loudly to the congregations, and these were now mostly abolished. In Wales, even more than in England, people were reluctant to give up these old ways which had entered deeply into their lives. Now at least the language of the readings and of the canticles and psalms, in which the congregation could join, began to make the people feel more at home in this new liturgy of the Church.

So William Morgan worked. Single-handed he translated the whole Old Testament and revised the earlier translation of the New Testament and the psalms. He made use of the best contemporary translations in English and French, but he also constantly went to the Greek and Hebrew originals of the texts he was dealing with. Here the work of Pentecost was being continued. The New Testament has translation woven into its texture. Jesus and his disciples spoke in Aramaic, the Gospels had already been transposed into Greek before they were written down. Through the efforts of translators that pentecostal work is carried on today.

The words of the Saviour, his call 'come, follow me', his command 'do this in remembrance of me', are words which come alive in the midst of the Church's worship, for as Luther says 'the Church is a mouth-house' not a 'pen-house'. In Welsh this involved the combination of common, beautiful prose with the princely language of the bards. The texts of the Bible are both poetry and prose, and William Morgan used all his genius as a writer to allow the old pre-Reformation tradition of sacred poetry to make its full contribution to the sonority of his biblical translations. This is particularly the case with the Old Testament prophets and the psalms. Here we see something of the underlying continuities of the Welsh tradition even in a moment of great discontinuity. Welsh was not, in the sixteenth century, as many Western European languages were, a language being newly formed and developed, it was a language which already had a long history of use in God's praise.

Gwenallt felt strongly about the recent past no less than the distant past. As a poet he can write not only in praise of bishops who were poets and scholars, but also of farmers and farm workers who could also be poets and scholars. He was a small man physically, full of energy and life, full of humour and a subversive sense of the ridiculous, quick too to be moved to passionate anger when he saw injustice. We find these qualities in one of the best known of his poems, 'Rhydcymerau' (*Translations*, no. 12 pp. 114–17), in which he celebrates the members of his own family who had worked the land of Carmarthenshire and in which he denounces the policies of a government in London whose purposes seem either military or commercial. It was a government which in the years after the Second World War already showed itself culpably ignorant and unconcerned about the human, social and cultural realities of life in small rural communities.

Some might complain that 'Rhydcymerau' is too nostalgic and too narrowly focused. But it might be replied that a man has not only a right but a duty to remember and be grateful for the lives of his own immediate fore-bears, and to protest against the tendency of distant bureaucracies, whether in government departments or in the headquarters of multinational companies, to be unaware of the true riches and values of human life. It is easy to destroy small rooted human communities; it is not at all easy to bring them to life again.

Gwenallt was very far from being merely nostalgic in his attitude towards the countryside. Sometimes he proves himself uncannily prophetic, as we see in a poem called 'The Earth' written well before concerns about ecology had become widely acknowledged and understood:

How intimate was the earth in days gone by,
As intimate as a neighbour, and fluent in the Welsh
   dialects;
We kept her in good shape, and we brought forth her
   colours
The colours of wheat, barley and oats;
We put a wave in her hair with the ploughshare,
And combed its sheen with the clanking harrows:
To the romantic ears of city poets
The bubbling brook was a distant yearning,
And in lonely mountain retreats
They built hospices fit for angels between two worlds.

The earth has been converted into a vast laboratory,
The cowshed into a factory where cogged cattle chew
   the cud;
No longer do the haughty bulls come
To mount cows on heat in the farmyard;
Their time-honoured dung-heaps have disappeared,
An alien chemistry is making the soil barren.

The earth no longer speaks man's homely language:
Her speech has a machine's syntax; the grammar of x,
   y, z:

The neighbour has become a distant monster; a
   monster whose hydrogenous jaws
Are about to swallow the husbandry and civilisation
   of man.

Pylons where once were angels
And the concrete damming the brook.[3]

In this poem Gwenallt identifies himself with the farmer
much more than with the poet, whose romantic and some-
what distant view of nature is treated with amused irony.
The world of nature is seen as a near neighbour to be
treated with respect and indeed affection, but also with
down-to-earth realism. The ideal which he admires is one
of an active collaboration between humanity and the world
around, a collaboration which has as its here unspoken
presupposition, the dependence of both man and nature
on the sustaining power of God the creator.

For Gwenallt, as we have seen, the new world of industry
and the old world of agriculture cannot be separated. Both
were an integral part of his own experience, and with the
development of agricultural machinery the one was beginning more and more to influence the other. The way in
which, in his poetry, he combines rural and industrial
images with distinctly religious motifs, can be found again
in an altogether different medium, in the work of a number
of South Wales' painters of this same period.[4] They were
artists who studied in the Swansea School of Art in the
years immediately before and after the First World War,
and who came from a very similar working-class background to that of Gwenallt. 'All the new painters came
from the western edge of the coalfield, where the rural
and the industrial continued to interact as they had done
throughout the nineteenth century. The non-conformist
tradition mediated through the Welsh language remained
strong. The imagery of Evan Walters and Archie Griffiths
in particular reflected this mixed culture.'[5]

Thus rural landscapes, industrial scenes, religious images, are all juxtaposed in their work; sometimes this is done more skilfully and sometimes less, but often in ways which recall Gwenallt's characteristic poems. In a large fresco painting by Archie Griffiths, in the Working Men's College in Camden Town in 1932, 'at the centre of a landscape of factories and fields, where agriculture and fertility were represented by a man tending his allotment in the company of a mother and child, Griffiths set a crucifixion. Christ's suffering ... was accompanied by symbols of the suffering of working people. Below the ground a miner was seriously injured in an accident, and at the other end of the mural a woman lay on her sick-bed, surrounded by her family as the doctor left the house.'[6]

But it is perhaps in the work of the oldest member of the group, Evan Walters (b. 1893), that the similarities to Gwenallt's use of imagery, socialist and Christian, industrial and rural, is most striking. Walters is a painter who can handle visual imagery with great power. It is clear from his paintings that he was intensely aware of the analogies between the sufferings of the working people in the 1920s and the passion of Christ. But how exactly did he understand that relationship? There is sometimes an ambiguity in the way in which he uses this imagery. This is particularly the case with a painting called *'The Communist'* which shows an orator standing on a soap box above a crowd, his arms wide outstretched in the form of a cross. Peter Lord comments 'Walters clearly suggested by the cruciform posture of the central figure in *'The Communist'* that the two were related, implying a denial both of Christianity and Marxism.'[7]

As we shall see in the following essay, such an identification of the communist and the Christian message did not, for Gwenallt, necessarily imply a denial of both. Rather for him it might suggest a positive interaction or indeed a kind of identification between them. The relationship between the work of Evan Walters and Archie Griffiths on the one side, and the development of Gwenallt's poetry from the romantic medievalism of his early writings, 'The Monk' (1926), and 'The Saint' (1931), to the realism of his mature work, has yet to be examined. There are similarities here which demand further investigation.

So far we have been allowing Gwenallt to lead us on a journey of discovery into aspects of the world of Wales, as he understood and experienced it, in the first half of the twentieth century. He has shown us not only vivid glimpses of the rural heartland of Wales but also the industrial areas of the south. He has suggested something of the interaction between them. We have seen something both of the clarity and the strength of his poetry, his capacity to say much in a brief space, to use unexpected images with unexpected force. Commenting on this quality of strength, Tony Conran remarks, 'When you translate him, you become aware of how massive he is, how his language has a physicality even with abstract words which reminds one of Ted Hughes, however different they are in other respects. And, above all there is his clarity of vision.'[8] Writing of his last collection of poems, published posthumously in 1969, Idris Foster remarks 'They reveal the strength and restraint of Gwenallt's later poetry, the masterly handling of craft and medium, the profound compassion – "in suffering there is depth, and this depth draws men, women and children together, close to one another . . ." as he says in *Aberfan* – and the undimmed vision.'[9]

II

Caro est salutis cardo; The flesh is the hinge of salvation

Gwenallt's autobiographical essay, *Credaf (I Believe)*, published in 1943, is a remarkable document in many ways.[10] It gives the impression of a man, at that stage in his middle forties, who has lived his life under constant inner pressure, a man with a quick, intuitive mind, a mind which veers from one point to another, and is not too troubled at holding a number of incompatible positions simultaneously. H. A. Hodges remarks of him, 'His writings come straight up out of the tensions of the society around him, which were fought out vividly in his own soul; between the rural culture of Wales and the industrialism, between Wales and England, nationalism and imperialism, pacifism and passionate revolt, Christianity and Marxism, socialist theory and the actualities of human life.'

If we look, for instance, at the moment in 1917 when he refused military service, we can see in his motivation elements of Christian pacifism, international socialism and nascent Welsh nationalism, deeply impressed by the Dublin rising of Easter 1916. If we look at his account of himself as a student in Aberystwyth six or seven years later, we find him passing through a phase of ardent aestheticism. 'Walter Pater was our master . . . and his book, *The Renaissance*, particularly his final section, was our Bible.' But he could not commit himself wholly to such a cult of art for art's sake, however attractive he found it. He had too much social conscience for that. 'Tolstoy was in my subconscious, with Dostoevsky, Marx and Lenin; with the poverty, pain, strikes and rebelliousness of south Wales; and my nostrils remembered the unnatural smell of the coffins

15

in the front parlours of workers' houses.' Here again he found himself holding in tension contradictory movements and contradictory positions.

In 1929, as a young lecturer in Welsh at the University in Aberystwyth, he tells us 'I went to a summer school in Spideal, a hamlet near Galway, to learn Irish'. There he acquired a new awareness of the value of language and of the value of the culture and traditions of rural life. Suddenly he had a new vision and a new understanding of the tradition which he had seen so unselfconsciously alive in the culture of his Carmarthenshire boyhood.

> Our country fathers' way of thinking – their interest in literature, theology, and tradition, their pride in family, ancestry and community – was completely different from that of the Marxist ... To a Marxist the past counted for nothing: only the present and especially the future ... It is true that I lectured on Welsh literature, but the history and literature of the Welsh past were no more to me than relics in a museum. To the Irish the past was a life-giving spring.

Reading the essay *Credaf* one feels that this moment in his life was for Gwenallt a decisive turning point. It is so in the text itself. Up until this point he has been taking us more or less chronologically through the growth of his convictions, and the various influences, intellectual and literary, which have caught his attention. Now something changes, and the last pages of the essay are devoted to an account of how he has gradually been able to reappropriate his Christian heritage, in a new way and with a new explicitness, and how he has sought to find his way towards a position which would do justice to the fullness and balance of Christian tradition, to do justice to the rightful claims of reason and nature as well as of faith and revelation. 'I set out' he says 'to make contact with the past, and although I am neither philosopher nor theologian I began to take an interest in philosophy and theology.'

He began from where he was, from the subject he was already teaching at Aberystwyth, from the literary tradition of Wales, which before he had thought of as a relic in a museum but which he now discovered to be a living source. Here at once he came across a contradiction. How was he to reconcile Dafydd ap Gwilym's humanism and Pantycelyn's theology? How was he to reconcile time with eternity, this world with the next, understanding with revelation, faith with reason? He thought that Kierkegaard and Barth would help him; and they did up to a point. He was delighted by 'their condemnation of the last century with its liberal theology . . . its faith in man's progress and development . . . its forgetfulness of sin.' But their reaction was too extreme, it had become one-sided. They rejected not only sin but man's mortality, and not only his mortality but his reason and understanding as well.

> Recent theology places too much emphasis on the biblical and Hebraic elements within the Christian tradition and neglects the Greek elements. The word 'humanism' is ambiguous. By humanism they mean man's belief in his ability to perfect himself without the aid of grace, his faith in his self-sufficiency, his attempt to deify himself; secular humanism. But true humanism is the humanism which makes room for understanding and reason as well as for grace, for the beauty of nature, for the arts and sciences, the co-operation between man and God, and God is the central point of such humanism, Christian humanism.

This is a theocentric humanism which recognizes the image and likeness of God in man and the possibility of our human response to God, on the basis of our creation in that image and likeness.

But the likeness and image of God is a gift of creation, and although the image has been soiled and trampled upon by sin, the sin of trying to be a god, yet it has not been annihilated. It is true that it is God in his salvation, his forgiveness and his grace, who comes to man, but it is also equally true that man has to discover his own sin and it is in doing that that he discovers the broken image of God in himself. God does not pour his grace into a man's heart as into an empty, dirty bucket; man's heart is like a garden; repentance cleans the thorns and briers and uproots the weeds which choke the seeds and shoots of goodness; grace then feeds them with sunshine, dew and rain. Grace perfects nature.

For Gwenallt the rediscovery of a sense of sin, as he had found it in the poetry of Baudelaire, was of absolutely vital significance. We see in this passage more clearly, why this should be so, because for him the sense of sin was not only a sense of guilt; it not only involved a sense of alienation from God, it also carried within itself the sense of a possible relationship with God, in the discovery that we are made in God's image and likeness. 'Whoever discovers his own sinfulness is already half a Christian' as he wrote, in words which are more fully taken up in the second part of this book. It is precisely because the potential of that divine image and likeness is there within us, that we feel so intensely the separation which sin makes between us and God. So Gwenallt concludes, we need this world and the next world, we need nature and grace, the divine and the human, not one or the other, but both together. Gwenallt sees the danger of an opposition between nature and grace, between flesh and spirit, not only as present in theology but also in much philosophy. 'This dualism is also present in modern philosophy. Descartes separated the body from the soul, and being separated *the body becomes a machine and the soul an abstraction. Mechanistic materialism grew from the one and abstract spiritualism from the other.*' [my italics]

For Gwenallt, with his new sense of the importance of history, there comes a new understanding of the value of pre-Reformation tradition, both in literature and theology. Here, he says, it is St Thomas Aquinas who shows us a better way, who makes room for all human faculties including the senses, in the human approach to God. 'He does not have the dualism of soul and body. He shows that faith and reason are both necessary and complementary to one another.' Gwenallt is delighted to find Dr Lewis Edwards, the greatest scholar of mid-nineteenth-century Welsh Methodism, commenting with approval on Aquinas as a theologian. We are here dealing, he implies, with matters which are common property to classical Christianity.

In this part of his essay, Gwenallt seems to be packing a vast amount of reading and reflection into a small space. The ideas follow on one another with excessive rapidity. It is therefore all the more striking that at this very point he makes an extended quotation from Clement of Alexandria, (c. 150–c. 215), in which the latter, arguing with the artists of ancient Greece, asserts that God alone as creator is the true, supreme artist. What is more, in creating the human person in his own image and likeness God has created the body as well as the soul. We see how vital it is for Gwenallt, who is himself an artist, with all the keenness of sensory perception which goes with that calling, that the bodily senses themselves should be known as God-given, with a potential for transfiguration into the divine likeness, so that the bodily senses too may become Spirit-bearing. In Clement's teaching he finds, he tells us, perhaps surprisingly, 'the best critique I have found of Pater's aesthetic doctrine and modern irrational naturalism'. These are views which in different ways see the joys of the senses, the joy of the body as being ends in themselves. But the true joy which we have in this world, the true joy which the body brings to us, points us beyond this world, to the mystery of the transfiguration of the senses, to the strange promise of the resurrection of the flesh. The true joy of the body is to be found, in the end, in God himself. Only in him does human life, and that includes bodily life, find its ultimate fulfilment.

So it is that in one of the greatest of his sonnets Gwenallt can proclaim

God has not forbidden us to love the world,
And to love man and all his works,
To love them with all the naked senses,
Every shape and colour, every voice and every
  sound.
There is a shudder in our blood when we see the
  trace,
Of his craftsman's hand upon the round creation,
And a ferment, when we cry out in mad triumph
That we do not want a life like this life.
And when the spirit leaves its robe of flesh
Folded stiff and cold in the coffin,
Surely it will come sometime on its journey
To put it on again like a robe of honour;
To take to itself the body, its nostrils and sight and
  hearing,
To make sensuous the glories of God. (see pp. 50–1)

This is an expression of Christian faith which allows the Biblical and Hebraic elements the very fullest expression, but which also allows place for its Greek elements. Something of this is to be seen in the remarkable sonnet, 'Venus and the Virgin Mary', which is quoted by Densil Morgan (see p. 52f.). Certainly the figure of Mary has replaced that of the pagan goddess of beauty, but in that radical transition nothing of value has been lost, the earlier vision has been transposed into another and eternal key.

In ways of which he was perhaps not always fully aware, Gwenallt was being drawn close to an Eastern Orthodox view of the Christian faith. He rejects 'the Roman Catholic tendency to make the Church synonymous with God's kingdom' and to confine Christianity to one culture, the Latin culture, when in fact it is to be incarnated in all human cultures. He sees in the Greek world potentials which the Latin world does not fully possess. Above all he insists 'Christianity is above every culture, every nationalism and every civilisation, but it ought to be within them like the lamps inside Gideon's pitchers.' Through the fleshly dress of particular cultures, particular languages, the one glory of the gospel is to shine out in a multiplicity of ways, for the gospel 'does not express a dualism between this world and the next, between flesh and spirit, between prayer and works'.

There is indeed a tension between this world and the world to come, between God's presence and work in creation as its creator and sustainer, and his presence and work as redeemer and judge, bringing all things to consummation. 'The kingdom grows like a mustard seed in this world, it also comes like a thief in the night from the mysterious other world.' Christianity is necessarily and always this-worldly and other-worldly. It comes to us as a gift from beyond; yet it is present at the heart of the world in which we dwell.

We are not surprised to find that Gwenallt turns to the moment of the transfiguration, that incident in the Gospels which is so central to the thought and prayer of the Christian East, in order to express the fullness of his own vision at this point. 'On the mountain of the transfiguration the unity of the deity and the humanity within it, the natural and the supernatural, were turned into a miracle like sunlight, whose brightness threw a bright cloud of mystery over the disciples.' The disciples must indeed descend from the mountain to face the doubt and suffering of the human condition. The end is not yet given in its fullness. Here we live still in a world full of imperfections. 'Christianity does not conceal the grave, but faces and conquers it. The rejoicing of Christ's Gospel is the rejoicing of the resurrection, the resurrection of the body. The sepulchre after all only retained possession of a napkin, and neatly folded linen cloths.'

There follows a remarkable passage in which Gwenallt seeks to sum up the fullness of the gospel mystery as he has come to understand it, with its many different sides and aspects.

> Christianity is the fellowship of the crib, the fellowship of the transfiguration, the fellowship of the last supper, of the garden, the cross, the resurrection, the ascension and the second coming. The three things essential to the Gospel are the crib, the cross and the empty tomb. We can look at the two pieces of the cross, the vertical piece is like an image of the relationship between God and man, man down below as a sinner, and God above him as the loving father, and the horizontal piece is the relationship between man and man, half of it an image of the sciences and half of the arts, and the wounded body holding together the two pieces in one cross. But the meaning of the cross depends on faith in the resurrection. It was in the light of the resurrection that St Paul and the Apostles interpreted the cross.

We have seen in this section Gwenallt's strong attraction to the Alexandrian element in early Christian thinking. But it is a Latin theologian of the same period, an almost exact contemporary of Clement's, Tertullian, (c. 160–c. 225), a very different kind of thinker from him, who can give us perhaps the best short summary of Gwenallt's deepest discovery about the nature of the faith. *Caro salutis est cardo*, it is the flesh which is the hinge of salvation. All turns on that.

This sense of the vital role of the flesh in the whole Christian scheme of things is expressed with unequalled force in one of Gwenallt's finest short poems, 'The Body of Christ'.

Hands like these hands
Were hammered to the tree:
Feet like our feet
Were pierced:
A head like ours
Bore the mocking thorns.

Such was your honour, such your rejoicing O flesh
In giving a body to the Son of God.
The body of a Jew in Bethlehem,
The mortal body of humankind,
The body transfigured in the grave into a living
    catholic body. (see p.80)

In taking our flesh God the Word takes on all the particularity, all the limitation of time and place, 'The body of a Jew in Bethlehem'. In taking our flesh God the Word takes on the mortality of the whole of humankind, the humanity which is enslaved by sin, subject to death, in alienation from God and from all creation. It is this body nailed to the cross, and placed in the tomb, which is there transfigured into a living body, a body wholly catholic, a body of all time and all place. This is the body which is raised on the third day, transfigured in the tomb.

Here surely there is a suggestion that as we need to read the account of the transfiguration in the Gospels, in the light of the death and resurrection that is to come, so we need to read the accounts of the empty tomb and the appearances of the risen Jesus in the light of the story of the transfiguration. Both the continuity and the discontinuity of Holy Saturday can be perceived here in a new way. Here we are helped to see further into the mystery to which Gwenallt constantly returns, of the way in which that which is altogether particular, of one time and one place, becomes altogether catholic, of all time and all places.

III

Intersection Places of the Timeless with Time

In our study of *Credaf* we have seen Gwenallt working his way towards a statement of the mystery of Christ in all its fullness and equilibrium. It is a statement which does justice both to the particularity and the universality of God's work in Christ. It is a statement which is at once catholic and evangelical, which clearly acknowledges the absolute centrality of the cross in any truly Christian faith and life and which knows from inside the meaning of the great affirmations of the Reformation, about God's free grace and our justification by grace, through faith alone. It is above all a way of seeing the Church which involves a qualitative rather than a quantitative understanding of catholicity.

> For Gwenallt the principle of the incarnation is to be seen at work in all things. That means that the universal and the particular for him are always held together. He had a vision of the Church as at once Catholic and local, rooted and free. As Idris Foster puts it, 'in his later poems Gwenallt's precise, as-a-matter-of-fact naming of persons and places – it is an old feature of Welsh poetry – is particularly noticeable.' The exactness of his topography is fused with the universality of his vision.[11]

This qualitative catholicity, this coinherence of the universal and the particular is to be found in two of Gwenallt's contemporaries who, coming from very different starting points found themselves making very similar affirmations. One of them, T. S. Eliot, has often enough been mentioned in connection with Gwenallt, though as yet no detailed study of their difference and similarity has been made. The other, a Russian Orthodox theologian from Paris, Vladimir Lossky, has not hitherto been considered in this particular connection.

I will look at these three writers together. But first we need to look more closely at this understanding of qualitative catholicity which allows us to hold the universal and the particular together, and which in different ways we find in all three writers. In this inward understanding of catholicity, the word 'catholicity' itself does not refer primarily to the Church's extension through space and time. Rather it refers to the fullness and integrity of the Church's life and being. The Church everywhere is constituted *kath holon*, according to its wholeness, in such a way as to reveal both its necessary particularity and its necessary universality. Each local church is not so much part of a larger whole, as itself an embodiment of the larger whole. Just as each believer, in principle, contains the whole Church within himself, so each local church is the whole Church in that place.

This is a vision represented in the Protestant world by the Congregationalist and Baptist traditions with their insistence on the rights and duties of the local gathered church. In Eastern Orthodoxy it is developed by the school of eucharistic ecclesiology which stresses the essential equality of every duly constituted local church, here understood as the diocese gathered around its bishop. In this case the complementary doctrine of the necessary communion which should bind the bishops of the Church together across time and space, assures universality as well as particularity. In such a vision of things, which is to be found throughout Christendom in the first millennium, there is room for the primacy of certain apostolic sees, but it is a primacy which functions within the college of bishops, not over and above it.

From such a standpoint, which is characteristic today of

the families of Eastern Orthodoxy, both Chalcedonian and non-Chalcedonian, and also of those Reformation churches which have retained the traditional episcopal structure, the new emphasis given to the theory and practice of collegiality during the Second Vatican Council was a development of very great promise. The more recent tendency in Rome, to draw back from that development, to reassert the authority of Rome over the college of bishops, the tendency in practice to make the bishops subject to the authority of the departments of the Roman Curia, when seen in this perspective, is nothing less than tragic. It certainly sets back the prospects of the restoration of Christian unity. It seems, at least to those who look from beyond the Roman communion, to imply a denial of the Church's true nature as diverse as well as united, as growing and flourishing in the multiplicity of languages and cultures which characterize the people of God, a multiplicity which itself reflects the exuberant richness of God's creation.

The curse of Babel is reversed not by the creation of a uniformity of life and language, but by a communion of different peoples with different stories, in which one hears 'in their own tongue' the wonderful works of God. This coinherence of unity and diversity in the Church of God has consequences which run through the whole of human society. It is a striking fact that this vision of diversity in unity and unity in diversity should have so seized the mind of three writers as different in their circumstances as Gwenallt, Eliot and Lossky, in the very same years at the beginning of the 1940s when the whole fabric of the old European world was shaken and in turmoil.

Each of these writers, from their very different viewpoints, found themselves called to reaffirm the meaning and identity of the history of the people to which they belong, not in isolation from other nations but in communion with them, and to make this affirmation by an appeal to the understanding of the Church as the communion of saints. This is a communion in which particular times and places are drawn together into one without losing their own particular qualities. They all find in that doctrine, in moments of almost catastrophic crisis and change, a way of affirming their faith in the presence and power of God in human history, a presence which saves humankind from the uttermost consequences of its folly. In their faith in the communion of saints they found as Pavel Florensky constantly affirmed in the revolutionary changes of Soviet society, that, 'the past has not passed away'. God who was with his people in the past is with them still.[12]

In the history of a people, in the history of a particular Church, there are moments in which time and eternity seem to coincide and interact. Eliot called them moments of the intersection of the timeless with time. Of such moments the lives of the saints are outstanding examples, the lives of the saints, understood not as relics to be preserved in a museum but as unfailing sources of light and insight for today. The sense of the nearness of eternity to time to be found in such lives, a sense which is particularly strong in the places where they lived and died, is characteristic of all three writers. For them time is fulfilled when it is transcended, as Eliot puts it in a preliminary note for *The Dry Salvages*, 'To get beyond time and at the same time deeper into time. The Spirit and the Earth.'[13]

We begin then from the point that all three writers affirm together, that it is in and through such lives that the life and history of a whole nation is most fully expressed. In such lives, which go beyond history, history itself is established and made sure. The lives of the saints, by providing moments at which time and eternity may meet and interact, give to the history of a people its meaning and direction. As Eliot writes:

> . . . a people without history
> Is not redeemed from time, for history is a pattern
> Of timeless moments.[14]

It is these timeless moments, these moments of intersection of the timeless with time, which give not only meaning and direction but ultimately redemption to the story of a people, buying back the moments of disaster and despair, buying back the moments of destructiveness and tragedy. Here the mere passage of time is transformed into a coherent story which proves to be in the end a revelation of God's love.

> For wherever a saint has dwelt, wherever a martyr has
>   given his blood for the blood of Christ,
> There is holy ground, and the sanctity shall not depart
>   from it . . .
> From such ground springs that which forever renews
>   the earth
> Though it is forever denied.[15]

Eliot celebrates this mystery most directly in relation to the martyrdom of the archbishop in *Murder in the Cathedral*. But the theme is also central in *Four Quartets* and in particular in the last of them, *Little Gidding*, where he commemorates one of the holy places of England, a place which he came to value above all in the years 1941–42 in which the poem was being written. These were years in which the very future of England was threatened as it had not been for centuries. In such a situation Eliot finds he can tell us much of the meaning of a holy place and of its significance for a whole nation.

> . . . you are not here to verify,
> Instruct yourself, inform curiosity
> Or carry report. You are here to kneel
> Where prayer has been valid. And prayer is more
> Than an order of words, the conscious occupation
> Of the praying mind, or the sound of the voice
>   praying.
> And what the dead had no speech for, when living,

They can tell you being dead; the communication
Of the dead is tongued with fire beyond the language
    of the living.
Here the intersection of the timeless moment
Is England and nowhere. Never and always.[16]

In this moment of the intersection of time and eternity
the barriers which separate the past from the present are
overcome, the past becomes present to us. In his poem
Eliot evokes two particular periods of great significance in
the history of England, the fourteenth and the seventeenth
centuries. The fourteenth century is present in the poem
through the quotations from two of its greatest spiritual
writers, Julian of Norwich and the author of *The Cloud
of Unknowing*. The seventeenth century is present through
the place Little Gidding itself, the home of the Ferrar
family, the place of their experiment in community living
which took place in the years before the Civil War, and
which so impressed contemporaries that both enemies and
friends saw it as a kind of monastery. So in calling to mind
these two times, and this particular place, Eliot is enabled
to make an affirmation about the whole history and meaning of the people with whom he had come to identify
himself.

> . . . so while the light fails
> On a winter's afternoon in a secluded chapel
> History is now and England.[17]

Eliot's appeal to the witness and presence of the saints
as providing purpose and direction for the life of a whole
nation can be paralleled in a very interesting way in the
work of Vladimir Lossky, and in particular in a recently
published work which was written in 1940.

Eliot had come from the middle-west of the United States
of America and settled in England and identified himself
with that country. Vladimir Lossky had come to the West

as an exile from Soviet Russia, expelled in 1922, settling in Paris in 1924 and adopting French nationality in 1938. In the June of 1940 at the time of the complete collapse of the French army, when his family had already taken refuge in the south of France, Vladimir Lossky set out on foot from Paris seeking to enlist in whatever French forces still survived. The diary that he kept during the seven days which he spent on the roads of France, walking, hitch-hiking, occasionally catching a train, travelling with a mingled crowd of refugees and fleeing soldiers, was written up in the following week. First published in 1998 it is a fascinating document, full of reflection on the history and calling of France, the country of his adoption. The parallels with Eliot are very striking.[18]

At this moment of disaster and despair he sees the history of France still present and embodied in the lives of its saints, in particular of two women saints. St Geneviève of Paris from the first centuries (*c.* 422–*c.* 500) and St Joan of Arc from the high Middle Ages (*c.* 1412–*c.* 1431) who continue to intercede for their compatriots. At this time of disintegration, he looks back and sees in the history of France 'a harmony in time, a continuity of life . . . a living duration which is always re-establishing links between past and present'. He sees the generations of pilgrims making their way towards the holy land, in search of the place where the apostles walked, he sees the knights and the kings setting out in search of the holy grail. 'Above all this land was made holy, from the first centuries, by the blood of the martyrs and the constant prayers of the saints.'

As a scholar and intellectual, the forced displacements of his life from Eastern to Western Europe had caused him to reflect on the meaning and nature of national identity. In the years of Hitler's Germany it was impossible to be blind to the dangers of a pagan and totalitarian national-ism. Lossky is very anxious to distance himself from any kind of nationalism which sees the individual as conse-quently simply swallowed up in 'the soul of the nation'.

He is very anxious too to distance himself from any kind of nationalism which simply sets one nation in opposition and hostility to another, or proclaims the superiority of one over another.

For him a nation is formed of human persons, called by God to share freely in the life of their people, and to take their responsibility for that life.

> The soul of the people is made out of our acts of heroism and our acts of cowardice, of our righteousness and of our sins, of our deeds of life and our deeds of death. Formed by millions of free wills, this structure of a people, ordained by the divine will, strengthened on its way by the saints – by those who walk in the way of God and who always watch over their people – this soul of a people, this non-organic structure, is always being formed, always in the process of becoming, always dependent on our acts and our decisions.[19]

Thus he sees the Christian calling of a particular people, a particular nation, not in isolation from others but as an element within the life of the whole people of God. Like Eliot and Gwenallt, Lossky is determined to be a catholic Christian, one who participates in the fullness of the universal Church but always in a way which respects and expresses the particular gifts and callings of particular peoples.

> France follows, it is true, the religious destiny of the Latin world; but it always keeps deeply rooted in its being, the latent tradition of Gallicanism. Now Gallicanism, in the most general sense of this word is nothing other than the defense of the rights of a local church, autonomous in its inner life, faithful to the ancient traditions of devotion and Christian culture which are proper to it. It is also a universalism, but a concrete universalism; it is formed in the diversity and richness

of the Christian lands, keeping their traditions, in the multiplicity of local churches, differing among themselves, which nonetheless constitute the One Holy Catholic and Apostolic Church. For the mystery of catholicity rests in the unity which is diversified and in the diversity which is united. There is no local catholicity, just as there is no abstract catholicity, apart from and above the local traditions.[20]

Here are the reasons which in the early 1940s prevented Gwenallt from becoming a Roman Catholic – and we may suppose Eliot too – the reasons which in 1957 drove him out of the communion of the Church in Wales, which in its chief bishop at that time seemed to be denying 'the ancient traditions of devotion and Christian culture which were proper to it'. Here, set out with theological clarity and precision is the position to which Gwenallt has been finding his way in *Credaf*. This is the context in which we need to put his own passionately held convictions about the inward catholicity of the tradition to which he belonged. It is not surprising that Lossky and Eliot, whose experience of life had been existentially and painfully uprooted and international, should approach this question with an analytical clarity which Gwenallt does not always reach. Nor is it surprising that he whose life had been lived in such deep and conscious communion with his own people, the small nation to which he belonged, should have had the gift to express these convictions with a vividness and a concreteness which sometimes escaped them.

Towards the end of his life, in a radio interview, Gwenallt expressed his conviction that the dust of the saints, from St David till today, lies in the land of Wales and makes it to be itself. He speaks not only of the saints of the earliest centuries and the Middle Ages, but of the saints of the Reformation period of the eighteenth-century revival and indeed of the nineteenth and twentieth century in his country. 'Our duty is to hand on the heritage we have received, to our children, a heritage of preaching the Gospel of the Son of God, of prayer and action and of forming in Wales a community on the foundation of the ethical principles of Christianity.' For him, as for Lossky, we have a responsibility for the handing on of this tradition which we have received. This tradition is not something anonymous and abstract, it comes to life in our living of it.

In Wales the great majority of the saints whose names are commemorated in the ancient parishes and villages of the land are men and women who are otherwise unknown. They are local figures, people of faith and prayers whose names are indissolubly linked with the particular places where their prayer was made valid. There is thus in Wales a special sense of the closeness of the saints and of their homeliness. There is also a strong sense of the New Testament emphasis that the call to holiness is a call to all who believe, a call to share in a common life and a common gift. So, in one of the greatest of his statements of this mystery of the saints of Wales, a poem which as the subsequent essay points out has in recent years attracted critical hostility as much as admiration, this affirmation of the ancient traditions of devotion and Christian culture which are the peculiar possession of his land, Gwenallt can celebrate the whole life and history of a believing people, the holy common people of God. Their life, their work, their prayer, their sorrow, their joy, their thanksgiving, all are touched by the transfiguring light of God, which in this poem he celebrates (see 'Wales', *Translations*, no. 4 pp. 98–9).

At one time I thought that this poem was too simplistic and too untroubled in its affirmation of the holiness of the land. Living with it longer and seeing it within the context of Gwenallt's work as a whole, a work which is as quick to see darkness as it is to see light, I have come to think that its serenity is anything but superficial. Not for nothing does it begin with the witness of the martyrs. It is a hard-won serenity which is celebrated here. As to the all-embracing quality of the poem's affirmation, that I believe may be rightly put alongside the no less striking declaration of the other David Jones, 'perhaps *Cymru* has no shrines because she *is* one'. This statement needs to be seen in relation to other statements in the essay of David Jones' from which it comes, in which he says 'those who read "The Stanzas of the Graves", the *Englynion y Beddau*, will understand how an actual topography, being commemorative, becomes inviolate, like a shrine'. Or again 'one is sometimes charged with a romantic rather than a realist attitude to these matters. But it is certainly no want of realism which makes one assert that the things of the *Cymry* are intricated in a rather special way with an historic language in an historic terrain.'[21] To compare the two David Jones, who despite their many differences share a common sense of the sacramental character of creation and the living presence of the past would surely throw new light on them both and their common commitment to the things of the *Cymry*.

IV

Towards a Conclusion

Gwenallt's poem, 'Wales', has a quality of great calm and serenity about it, things which are by no means always to be found in his writing. On the one side one finds at times joy and celebration, on the other side one finds anger, pain, bitterness and distress. The peace which is to be found in this poem is certainly not a peace of emptiness or complacency. It is a peace which has been won on the far side of much conflict.

This double quality in Gwenallt's work, this sorrow which brings joy, is very clearly to be seen in a number of photographs taken of him during the last months of his life. On seeing one of them, his friend and contemporary Euros Bowen at once exclaimed, 'He's got the marks on him', the marks of the cancer which was shortly to kill him. Certainly it is the face of a man deeply marked with suffering and illness. Yet as you look at it, the photograph reveals something else: first a sense of calm and peace, and then, even more surprisingly, a kind of quiet joy. This was my own quite spontaneous, altogether unprepared reaction to the photograph, when I first saw it on the sleeve of the LP recording of Gwenallt's reading of his own verse.

H. A. Hodges makes a comment on Gwenallt's work which is relevant at this point. It is a comment which at first I found myself inclined to disagree with. He says that Gwenallt's religious poems are 'neither solemn nor exuberant'. I had the impression that at times they could be both. Hodges goes on to say that his religious poems 'breathe a kind of quiet joy; a joy in mere existence, joy in God as the source of existence, joy in God's world, our place in it and the share which God himself has taken in our life here'. It is a sentence which deserves to be examined closely.

At the root of Gwenallt's verse there is joy and amazement, praise and thanksgiving for the very fact that anything exists at all. There is also joy at the mysterious fact that within and behind all existence there is God himself. Then there is amazement and joy in this world of ours as we know it, our familiar planet, our familiar environment, and with that a recognition that this world too is God's world as well as ours. This joy itself comes from the last and deepest source of our amazement and wonder, that is our discovery of the share which God himself has taken in our life here.

By entering into our world, into our humanity in the life of Jesus of Nazareth, God himself has become one with us, embodied in our flesh. From that central point of incarnation we can look backwards and forwards into the whole world of human history and see so many partial embodiments of God's love in such an immense variety of times and places. Above all we see this love in the lives of the saints and in particular in the lives of those who have given their lives as a costly offering of faith, meeting death often at its most violent and hateful, at the stake, in the concentration camp, with a hope and a love which is stronger than death.

All this is to be found in Gwenallt's verse in general and in this particular poem in a very special way. We see it in his way of linking what is human with what is divine, what is human with what is characteristic of existence as a whole, i.e. what is cosmic. We see it in his way of seeing at once the homeliness and the holiness, the particularity and the universality of God's presence when he comes 'to take a share in our life here'.

This vision of the closeness of God's presence with us is, as Bobi Jones remarks in his discussion of Gwenallt's work, 'the heart of the message both of evangelical and of sacramental christianity'.[22] This is a powerful evangelical catholic affirmation which has many ecumenical consequences, especially when we consider that its author is one who would be called a conservative evangelical, a writer who is an outstanding representative of the Augustinian-Calvinist tradition in Wales. But its implications go further still, as Bobi Jones also points out. By being so strongly earthed Gwenallt's vision also has strong ecological consequences:

> The picture we are given is of a land where the Gospel is a penetrating presence, a place where God shows himself able to meet with the earth personally. On this account there is a depth in our history, and a geography of special places throughout our land, which bear witness that God can act powerfully in places that are 'small' 'insignificant' 'out of the way' and this is a common background to us all.
>
> Therefore this nation, like many other nations, is like a sacrament; an object in which God embodies himself;

or for those who see it as an ordinance it is a visible sign of the hidden work of the one who is unseen. And perhaps we should add 'and only a sign' for the means of grace are not automatic nor do they contain grace within themselves. It is 'only a sign of grace', and yet of course, like every part of God's creation, it can also be a channel through which that grace is at work. All the same it is God alone who gives the blessing, but as through the sacraments, so through the manifestation of himself in the tradition of the nation and in the beauty of the world, testimony is borne. So through the heart which finds new birth and the dead spirit which receives new life, God makes a place for his grace and reveals himself in the history of a people.[23]

This understanding of Gwenallt I find to be profoundly perceptive and true; certainly it has great significance for Christian unity. But while recognizing its truth we should not neglect also to recognize its strangeness. It is strange in many ways, perhaps first of all in its quiet and confident affirmation of the innermost truth of the one Christian tradition, the truth that God became human, entered into our life, in order that we might enter into God's life in its fullness, that fullness for which we were made at the beginning, and in doing so in some way might bring with us the whole creation into the presence and the glory of God.

But it is strange too in its affirmation of the ecumenical significance of Gwenallt's work, its catholic-evangelical quality, its potential for bringing reconciliation between the divided Christian traditions. This is an affirmation which cannot and should not be made lightly. If we think of the fifteen hundred years of the history of the Church in Wales, in terms of an ecumenism in time we have to recognize that it is marked by the fatal split between East and West in Christendom which took place in the eleventh and twelfth centuries and which so impoverished both sides of the division. We have also to recognize the split between Rome and most of the churches of North and Western Europe which took place in the sixteenth century and which was for both sides at times terribly destructive in its effects. We have to think again of the wars of religion which followed in the seventeenth century and of the disruptions involved in the religious revivals of the eighteenth century. All this can, it is true, be brought together, and in some way it is being brought together in our own century, not least in the vision and prayer of poets like Gwenallt and Waldo and Saunders Lewis. But we have also to recognize that at a more public and official level this reconciliation is still little enough realized or embodied in the lives of our churches and communities.

And if this was true for Gwenallt, as he looked back on the history of Wales, how much more was it true for Vladimir Lossky, this Russian who had so wholeheartedly accepted France as his adopted country. As he walked through the disaster of June 1940, Lossky was not at all unaware of the paradoxical nature of his affirmation of the underlying unity, the divine-human unity, hidden at the heart of the history of France. Indeed, as a theologian he was intensely conscious of the specific nature of the Orthodox tradition to which he belonged. He often found himself obliged, in all conscience, to point to the profound differences which still exist between the separated Christian confessions of East and West, differences which were never for him a matter of indifference.

France, in its history, had participated fully in that eleventh-century schism which had broken the communion between Constantinople and Rome. The great gothic cathedrals, and the flowering schools of theology, above all in the University of Paris, demonstrated the revolutionary newness of what followed on from it in France. In the sixteenth and seventeenth centuries France had not avoided the conflicts of the Reformation nor the pains of the wars of religion or the persecution of Protestants. If there was a living unity within the French tradition, and between France and the Orthodoxy of the East, as he certainly felt there was, it was not yet something fully manifest. In Lossky, no less than in Gwenallt and in Eliot, we are speaking of a unity which is held in God's hands and not in ours.

It was the same for Eliot. In writing *Little Gidding*, he was concerned with a place indissolubly connected with the conflicts which led up to the Civil War in England, and with the hurts of that period, in which men and women of passionately held convictions found themselves in mortal opposition to one another, 'united in the strife which divided them'.

Commenting on that poem Donald Mackinnon insists that in one sense we can never align ourselves completely with any one of those past divisions. 'We cannot be partisan and follow an antique and silent drum. There is a kind of make-believe in trying to fight the battles of the past as if they were our own. Yet the answer to this attitude is not found in a sort of superior detachment, altogether disdainful of issues for which good men were prepared to die.' And Mackinnon speaks of a form of commitment which allows us 'to see how much we owe to those who are on the other side from that to which in some sense we have given our allegiance'. We have to learn to look beyond the narrow confines of the divisions as they were then envisaged, but at the same time we must not imagine we have found some easy or quick solution of all problems. 'Yet to talk in this way is not to commit ourselves to some vision of a synthesis in which reconciliation is achieved. Men died; others were banished and knew the loneliness of exile.' We may think in Wales of Rawlins White, John Penry, and the Catholic exiles of the later part of the sixteenth century. 'These sufferings were real enough; yet if we recall their reality it is not to summon up our animosity. Rather it is a remembrance that must have an ascetic quality ... I would suggest that in this poem we have an example of the attempt to present "the meaning of history". If that phrase has any sense, it may be the sort of thing that can only achieve its definition in poetry.'[24]

What Donald Mackinnon says there about Eliot's writing in the *Four Quartets* may surely also be said about Gwenallt's work, not only in the particular poem we have been considering, but in the body of his poetic work taken as a whole. We have in that work a consistent attempt to present something of the meaning of human history as it is seen in the light which comes from the mountain of transfiguration and from the cross and the empty tomb. As one who lived as a poet in and through *y pethe*, 'the things' of his nation, as it is said in Welsh, Gwenallt sought above all to discern the shape and meaning of its long history. It is the history of a small country, in that like Palestine; a history which has been marked by disasters, in that also like Palestine. In reading his work again we find ourselves in agreement with Mackinnon that this is a kind of meaning which can only find its definition in poetry.

But without necessarily being poets, we ourselves may be able to enter into that meaning in a great variety of ways. We can do it, for instance, by actually going on pilgrimage to a place where prayer has been valid, a place where perhaps above all in silence we may find that the past has not passed away. To visit such a place is itself an exercise in ecumenism in time; we discover the reality of the communion of saints which unites us across our differences. We can also do it by allowing ourselves to feel and understand, as Waldo does in his poems for the Catholic martyrs, something of the inwardness and courage of those with whom, historically, we should have been in conflict, by not running away from the pain and agony involved in that struggle.

We can also do it by coming to understand the many points of reconciliation between the divided Christian traditions which have actually been established in the ecumenical exchanges of the last forty years. If they have not yet brought us to a final resolution of our differences they have certainly brought us far along the way towards it. Above all we can ponder and celebrate as Gwenallt did, the example of the martyrs of the twentieth century, those Catholic, Protestant and Orthodox who have given their lives for their faith. Here in our time we are given perhaps the strongest sign of the mystery of this faith which unites Christians even now across their evident divisions. As Pope John Paul has said, we already have an ecumenical martyrology. In the calm courage with which they were able to meet the onset of death, a Dietrich Bonhoeffer, an Edith Stein, a Maximilian Kolbe, a Maria Skobtsova have revealed something of the healing power of 'a faithfulness without fanaticism, a hope based on facing the darkest reality, a love that transcended life itself'.[25] Here, in the midst of all the ambiguities of history, a way through, a paradoxical pattern of meaning seems to be given.

Writing this essay with an eye to the hundredth anniversary of Gwenallt's birth in 1999 has made me feel more strongly than ever that here is a man whose work can be of genuine and ground-breaking value for us in the new millennium. It gives us a new incentive to discern afresh the sense of the history of the different and conflicting peoples of this island, Welsh, English and Scottish, and a new courage to seek for ways of reconciliation and peace between the separated traditions of the one family of Christ.

I have found in Gwenallt's work, in some ways unexpectedly, a deep, hidden joy, a joy which comes from his faith in God's incarnation in our world 'the share which God himself has taken in our life here'. As he went on in life, as more and more the hymns of his childhood, with all their meditation on the cross, came back to him, Gwenallt found himself more and more dwelling on the mystery of God's presence with us in the midst of pain and loss, at the heart of human tragedy and defeat. He found himself meditating anew on the theme of God's compassion. This

was what Waldo Williams saw when in the months after
Gwenallt's death he came to write a poem in his honour.

> ... He had an hour's space,
> One incomprehensible hour and insight to see
> In the old paradoxes of our race,
> The strong Arms trembling in holy anxiety
> Under the world; and gave his gasping breath
> To the King of Heaven dying on the Cross.[26]

Gwenallt: Poet of Flesh and Spirit

D. DENSIL MORGAN

One of the key pieces of autobiographical prose written by any Welsh poet of the twentieth century was Gwenallt's essay *Credaf* (*I Believe*), published as an explicit contribution to Christian witness during the darkness of the Second World War. Not only did that essay illuminate so much of Gwenallt's own work, from the romantic aestheticism of his early eisteddfod odes 'Y Mynach' ('The Monk') (1926), 'Y Sant' ('The Saint') (1928) and 'Breuddwyd y Bardd' ('The Poet's Dream') (1931), to the much more mature and intellectually disciplined work contained in *Ysgubau'r Awen* (*Sheaves of the Muse*) (1939) and in the slim (and neglected) volume *Cnoi Cil* (*Thinking Things Over*) of 1942, but it also marked a clear phase in the development of the Christian consciousness in Wales. Apart, perhaps, from the wartime essays of the theologian J. E. Daniel, a more limpid, lucid expression of practical orthodoxy in Welsh cannot be found. On the one hand it showed how Christian faith interacted with the evils of the contemporary world in all their secular intractability, and on the other it made quite plain that the profession of Christianity demanded costly repentance and a clear faith, in fact nothing less than a wholehearted and definite conversion to God. When chapel culture was still dominant in Wales and nominal Christianity part of the social convention of the time, this unabashed claim was disconcerting to say the least. It was also bracing and hugely exciting. By nailing his colours to the mast, Gwenallt's witness challenged his contemporaries and, unbeknown to him, would challenge not a few of those who were not yet born.

My reason for beginning this essay by mentioning Gwen-allt's 1943 confession of faith is highly personal: it was through his conversion that my own, at least in part, came about. In a very real way his autobiography became a part of my own and his poetry came to express every conviction which I held and hold dear. I hope you will bear with me as I try to explain.

My home and all my family roots are in the lower Swansea Valley and that part of West Glamorgan between Morriston and Pontarddulais. I grew up in Morriston during the late 1950s and 60s in a home shared with my maternal grandparents. The house was cramped and terraced consisting of a kitchen, a living room and a front parlour with two upstairs bedrooms. Lacking a bedroom of my own I shared one with my grandfather. Small of stature and a typically Iberian Celt, he had spent his life working hard in the tinplate mills. I have a vivid memory of his returning from the day shift and putting his blue goggles on the kitchen table and showing me the marks where the sparks from the furnace had scratched the lenses. Only later did it dawn on me how harsh and dangerous his work had been. My childhood was, for the most part, very happy indeed, the only shadow being my parents' earlier separation (which, in those days, set me apart from virtually all my friends) though the love shown by my mother and grandparents made up for any psychological loss which I may have incurred. Like so many South Wales families of that time, chapel going was taken for granted as was attendance at Sunday School, Band of Hope and playing an active part in the monthly children's service on a Sunday morning. In a short-lived rebellious phase, I left our rather staid, solid and Welsh-speaking Baptist chapel for the much more exotic (and English-speaking) Pentecostal mission, but although for a ten-year-old the worship there was much more 'fun', I soon returned to the family paths. Religion was a part of life which it never occurred to me to forsake.

Adolescence was fairly painful. There is nothing odd about that but in my case it was made more painful still by an innate shyness (I was an only child), little sporting prowess and only moderate academic ability. Neither had I any experience of the company of girls. The huge single-sex comprehensive school to which I went was ghastly and for the most part I felt alienated and lost. There were, however, a few friends whose background was similar to my own and whose commitment to Wales was marked. By now the 1960s were in full swing and Welsh nationalism had become a popular, though still a minority, enthusiasm. By my fourteenth year I was already identifying myself not so much by my social class – about which there was no question anyway – but by nationality and culture. The Welsh that I possessed was colloquial, passive and altogether deficient (I had gone to the local infants and junior schools rather than the Welsh medium school some distance away) and from about then onwards I decided to learn Welsh thoroughly and by so doing to stake out my identity clearly. This I accomplished by my mid-teens; Welsh soon became not just the language which my grandparents habitually spoke with one another (though not, strangely, with my Welsh-speaking mother) but mine as well.

The subjects which I enjoyed in school were English, history and Welsh. (I was a complete dud at anything mathematical or scientific and, unfortunately, at the time, at French.) Milton and Wordsworth I could appreciate; also I had begun to get a feeling for the past; and then came Gwenallt. I cannot recall that his poetry was on the syllabus, but having begun to stray beyond the set books I happened upon his verse. It was little short of a revelation. Here was verse which was direct, masculine and craggy and highly relevant to modern life. What is more it was descriptive of the realities with which I had grown up. Gwenallt's sonnet 'Gweithwyr Deheudir Cymru' ('The

45

Workers of South Wales') in *Cnoi Cil* was, in fact, a portrait of my grandfather and his contemporaries, and his remarkable description of South Wales during the depression was redolent of a still vivid past:

> Men in South Wales without a drink or food or a fag,
> And the pride of their district under heaps of scrap,
>   cinders and slag:
> The canal stagnant in villages, without shout or
>   movement or sound
> And the pot-bellied rats ripping up the bodies of dogs
>   and cats.

'Ar gyfeiliorn' ('Astray'), *Ysgubau'r Awen* (*Translations*, no. 35
pp. 149–50)

(Once, when walking on the towpath of the Swansea canal in the company of my grandfather, I saw a huge rat ripping open the stomach of a dead cat.) This was not the poetry of books ('I wandered lonely as a cloud') but of experience, verve and everyday life. I had never come across anything like it before and it knocked me off my feet.

My baptism into the Christian Church had taken place when I was fifteen. It was (I hope) sincere, a conscious commitment to faith and discipleship which was, nonetheless, characterized by a woeful ignorance of doctrinal formulations and was also devoid of any deep emotional significance. For some months adolescent agnosticism jostled uncomfortably with a desire for spiritual certainty, but I persevered resolving not to give in to atheism or unbelief. What I did not realize was that God's absence was, in fact, a sign of his transcendent reality: 'Verily thou art a God that hidest thyself, O God of Israel, the Saviour' (Isa. 45:15). (When I read, years later, St John of the Cross's description of 'the dark night of the soul' – in Saunders Lewis' *Williams Pantycelyn* (1927) as it happened – I knew that I had been there before.) Slowly, but very really, God's relentless absence became a brooding presence which, in turn, became a call to Christian service through the ordained ministry within the Welsh Baptist tradition. If my faith, at this time, was real enough, it was still blighted by a titanic doctrinal ignorance. And then again, along came Gwenallt!

The Christian content of Gwenallt's verse is massive and blatant, yet it was not that but his searingly realistic descriptions of modern industrial Wales which first endeared him to me. But the more I read, the more overwhelming his Christian conviction became. What is more, it was the words of a sonnet of his which provided me with the key to understanding a particularly unnerving experience which I was undergoing at the time, the awesome experience of the conviction of sin. It was this, and all that followed from it, which made my Christian conversion complete ('Pechod' ('Sin'), *Translations*, no. 33 p. 147).

In his autobiographical essay Gwenallt had written of his pilgrimage from early agnosticism through atheism, Marxism, romantic aestheticism, Baudelairean decadence and eventually to Christian faith. C. S. Lewis, whose own conversion had coincided roughly with Gwenallt's, was later to muse: 'Amiable agnostics will talk cheerfully about "man's search for God". To me, as I was then, they might as well have talked about the mouse's search for the cat.'[1] Far from being an abstraction, God, for both of them, had become a dread-inspiring transcendent reality whose righteousness was both judgment and redemption. 'Whoever discovers his own sinfulness', said Gwenallt in that essay, 'is already half a Christian.'[2] That was the sentence which clinched it for me. From then on it all came together and I was launched on a voyage of faith in which Christian orthodoxy, evangelical in content and catholic in its wholeness, became my constant comfort, beacon and rationale and has remained so for a quarter of a century or so. It is in order to repay a debt of gratitude, therefore, that this essay has been composed.

I

Howling for the Blood of Redemption

One of the weaknesses of Puritanism, indeed of Western or Latin Christianity generally, is its tendency to begin with man's sin rather than with God's sheer and amazing grace. By so doing it can become one-sided, legalistic, obsessive and judgmental; there is no doubt that this is true of some kinds of evangelicalism and much of the Methodist tradition as well. So to begin this analysis with Gwenallt's discovery of sin is, potentially, a hazardous undertaking. Yet because of its underlying importance in his canon and in his own experience, that is where I will start.

Apart from the sonnet entitled 'Sin', there are two other poems in *Ysgubau'r Awen* which treat this theme directly and there are a host of references throughout the work where it is implied or understood. In the first poem, to the Twrch Trwyth, the mythical wild boar of Welsh medieval folklore, the creature becomes the symbol not merely of human fallenness and corruption but of the primitive evil which the poet himself shares in:

> He was formed of the blind passions
> In the soil of our base nature.

The poet's dilemma is that of everyone whose conscience has been awakened: 'For the good which I will, I do not; but the evil which I will not, that I do' (Rom. 7:19). No matter how hard he applies his will to pursue the beast in order, hopefully, to destroy it, its wiliness and its beguiling nature, 'the jewels between its ears/ Which excite our lust and greed', ensure its perpetual escape. Yet the beast's death is assured, not through the feeble and inadequate

48

willpower of the hunter but through the invincible grace of Christ manifest in and through his Church:

> When it puts its cruel, brutish head
> Upon her pure knee,
> I will strike it with my silver blade
> Until its blood runs free.

It is only thus that the human will is released from its bondage to accomplish that which, at its best, it has desired all along, resisting sin rather than succumbing to it and carrying through and celebrating its utter destruction.

The four stanzas of 'The Polecat' are even more virulent and the description of the animal is even more striking and ugly:

> I saw you staring impudent and greedy
> On a hillside so full of yourself,
> Your wretched corpus in the light of the sun
> Was like a blot of ink on a scroll.
>
> You quit your untamed family in the forest,
> The cats, the skunks and the hogs,
> And crossed the meadow to the homes of the people
> To pursue your bloody spoil.
>
> If only I had a two-barrelled shotgun
> And a cartridge in its breach,
> I would let fly and so bury death beneath your pelt
> And leap with ecstasy at your pain.
>
> You wouldn't sneak back like sin into the forest,
> Your kindred would see you ne'er again,
> But you'd lie as a corpse in all your stench,
> Like cold filth on the meadow floor.

'Y Ffwlbart' ('The Polecat')

My prosaic translation does scant justice to the carefully crafted original, its stark choice of words heightening its bold imagery. Its gleeful violence is intentional and was quite scandalous given the demure nature of so much Welsh religiosity during the 1930s. Gwenallt had no time at all for conventional pieties; his interest was in the reality of human corruption and in its corresponding need for radical surgery. The poem plumbed the depths which St Augustine among the Catholic Fathers and John Calvin among the Reformers would have appreciated only too well.

Human sinfulness for Gwenallt was an intractable and tragic reality wreaking havoc on the world simply because it was at work in everyone, no matter how virtuous or outwardly pious. His antipathy to the optimistic liberal theology of his day was due to its superficial analysis of the human condition and its inevitable inability to provide an adequate remedy for evil. The only hope of redemption was that God himself would descend into the abyss not only of humankind's finitude but of its evil and corruption in order to 'clear out all our filthy ditches/ And kill off all the impurities in our blood' ('Y Duwdod' ('The Godhead')). The theme of sinfulness is complemented and rightly overshadowed by that of redemption, a redemption made possible by God's incarnation and sacrificial atonement, his taking upon himself human flesh in order to provide that flesh with a means of overcoming the evil by which it has been infected.

A second rich and connected theme in *Ysgubau'r Awen* is that of spirit and the flesh. The sonnet 'Cnawd ac Ysbryd' ('Flesh and Spirit'),

God has not forbidden us to love the world,
And to love man and all his works,
To love them with all the naked senses,
Every shape and colour, every voice and every sound,

has already been quoted by Donald Allchin. It is justly famous as Gwenallt's most rounded description of the incarnational or sacramental principle which banishes all duality between the temporal and the spiritual realms and revels in God's affirmation of his own good creation. Though the flesh has been contaminated by the blight of sin and so shares in the inheritance of death, it is yet capable of being restored to become a vehicle for the true praise of God and for his service within human society and the world. The same theme is treated in other poems, especially 'Yr Angylion a'r Gwragedd' ('The Angels and the Women') and the sonnet to the hymn-writer and saint Ann Griffiths. But the tremendous crescendo in the closing couplet of 'Flesh and Spirit'

> To take to itself the body, its nostrils and sight and hearing.
> To make sensual the glories of God

sums up what was to be the poet's abiding conviction and the key to his Christian philosophy and practice.

In the early poems this glorying in the flesh and its sensuousness is connected with his still earlier near-libertine attraction to the flesh as symbolic of unrestrained carnality. Always a passionate man, during his undergraduate days Gwenallt had dabbled both with Marxism and also with a debauched aestheticism through which he had tried to rid himself of the repression of his puritan upbringing. Taking a leaf from Walter Pater's then fashionable handbook on the Renaissance, he had wanted to embrace life in all its vibrant fullness and to experience all things to excess. 'Intense emotion was what kindled life in us and sharpened our consciousness, especially the intensity of poetry, the love of beauty and art for art's sake', he wrote in his autobiographical essay. Marx had made way for Apollo and Dionysius, altruism for self-gratification understood virtually as a means of salvation. 'Why could we not be purely pagan like the Greeks', he continued, 'and slip from one joy to the next, from one passion to the next, and, in the end, fall joyfully satiated into the grave where there was no difference between a man and a sheep?'[3] Such a heady romantic nihilism could, of course, only lead to despair, as Baudelaire, the greatest and most dissolute of the nineteenth-century French poets had discovered. Curiously it was through Baudelaire (who, as T. S. Eliot had noted, was 'man enough to be damned') that Gwenallt himself discovered the potency of sinfulness, yet his feeling for the sensual quality of Greek life remained a powerful factor in his post-conversion experience. The splendid translations from poets of the Middle Ages, the Goliardi and François Villon in *Ysgubau'r Awen*, celebrate a glorious *joi-de-vivre* of wine, women and song which is nevertheless overshadowed by the dread inevitability of death, bearing witness to his ongoing interest in the subject. By now he had come to recognize that the only hope for the flesh was not its repression through a bloodless puritanism or its dissolution through a Hellenistic hedonism but its sanctification through God's taking it upon himself in Christ's incarnation and atonement. Like the wolves, humankind was forced to look skyward and bay for the blood of redemption.

The sonnet to Venus and the Blessed Virgin pits transient Hellenistic beauty against the eternal verities of the gospel and decides, unblushingly, in favour of the latter:

You stunned a world when you rose up from the
    waves
Whose spray was skin on flesh so smooth,
Every heart quickened in your presence
And even the aged had their tepid passions renewed;
Artistry carved, with chiselled mastery,
The image of your divinity in marble and stone,
And in your temple man's spring prostrated itself,
Virginity and harlotry both cried out before you.

The Mother of Sorrows and Heaven's Intercessor
Came forth from Bethlehem into your world on her
    journey,
Turning your temples into the temples of her Son,
And planting the cross where the altars of flesh had
    been;
She will stand forever where once you stood
With salvation resting between her arms.

'Fenws a'r Forwyn Fair' ('Venus and the Virgin Mary')

Just as Greek paganism had been swept away by the victory of Christianity during the fourth and fifth centuries, so even the most enticing temporal charm is forced to yield to the gracious compulsion of God's call. Gwenallt's terse *englyn* to Lazarus makes the same point, this time denoting the resurrection of the flesh, which, along with the incarnation, indicates God's acceptance and renewal of human finitude:

You escaped from the house of death, graveclothes
        Still wrapped around you,
And all of enlightened Greece witnessed
One who was mightier than Jove.

'Atgyfodiad Lazarus' ('The Resurrection of Lazarus')

The faith which Gwenallt professed in this earliest volume of verse is orthodox and catholic. Its sacramental quality is vouched for by the regard he has for Mary as *Theotokos*, the bearer of the Godhead, through whom Christ, as the eternal Logos, was conjoined with human flesh. The salvation which is offered in *Ysgubau'r Awen*'s most celebrated poem, 'Astray', which begins with the frequently quoted line 'Woe unto us who know the words without knowing the Word', is quite specifically catholic:

O Mary, set Your Star in the midst of heaven's
    darkness,
And show with your chart the path back to His will,
Come down between tangled ropes, put your hand on
    the helm,
And guide our obstinate ship to one of God's ports.

His sonnets to Ireland, to Dante, to the Nuns, and to
Saunders Lewis all express this real attraction to catholic
Christianity, as does his sonnet entitled 'Yr Eglwys' ('The
Church'):

When the stars oppress our flesh,
And their lofty antiquity fills us with awe,
It raises a fortress where our poor spirit
Can flee for refuge, as night falls, and bow its head;
And there we place at Your feet
The burden of our sinful insignificance,
The humble frailty of flesh and blood,
And dread at Your awesome creation.
But we see that it is from Your hand like a gentle
    spring
That all forms of life flow each in its time,
And that Your back is in the deep waters,
Your shoulders in the massive stability of the
    mountains,
The nebulae of the heavens and the countless stars
Are but the harmonious mantle of Your immortality.

Although no mention is made of the Virgin, the altar or
of the sacrifice of the Mass, it is clear that the Church is
envisioned here as a visible spiritual institution rooted in
time and place and not the more Protestant idea, familiar
from the poet's upbringing, of the invisible church or the
local fellowship of believers. (It was the Church, it will be
remembered, and not Christ as such *apart* from his Church,
through which the Twrch Trwyth would be enticed to

its death.) This attraction towards the catholic faith took Gwenallt not to Rome but to Anglo-Catholicism; he was confirmed as a communicant member of the Church in Wales at the Bishop of St David's Palace at Abergwili in 1944 and thereafter worshipped regularly in the ancient parish church at Llanbadarn. Yet there were already signs that he would be drawn back eventually to the Reformed faith which he found so irksome in his youth, or that he would at least devise a synthesis between the rich sacramentalism of catholic Christianity and a renewed appreciation of chapel culture and the theology of the Word.

The Wales to which he had, by the mid-1930s, become so passionately committed was, after all, still very much a Protestant, chapel-going Wales, and following the Methodist Revival it was Nonconformity which had left its mark so indelibly on the life of the nation during one of the most creative phases in its modern history, the industrial phase which was such an important element in his own background. Whereas as a young poet he had fallen under the spell of the incomparable T. Gwynn Jones and had rejoiced in the chivalry and romanticism of the medieval past, it was contemporary Wales, with all its industrial crises and political upheavals, with which he felt inextricably involved. Along with themes we have already considered, such as human sinfulness, the spirit and the flesh and Christianity's victory over the forces of corruption, another major theme in *Ysgubau'r Awen* is that of Wales itself. The six stanzas of the poem 'Gwlad Adfeiliedig' ('A Ruined Land') describe the plight of rural West Wales, the area which Gwenallt's parents had left a generation earlier in order to seek a better life in the industrial valleys, while the three poems, each entitled 'Cymru', illustrate the range of emotions which the poet felt for his country's current malaise. The first rather sweet lyric has undoubtedly suffered from over-use, but despite the frequently made charge of cliché and bathos, it is not devoid of solid content and its charm persists. 'There is one lovely poem', wrote H. A. Hodges of it, 'full of light and joy, in which Gwenallt expresses his dream of Christian Wales. The dust of all the saints of the ages is in her bosom; angels have trodden her roads and the Holy Dove has nested in her woods. Bards have heard in the wind the cry of Christ's passion.

> His resurrection was your spring,
> Your summer his verdant salvation
> And in the winter of your mountains
> He built tabernacles of grace . . .'[4]

Hodges's opinion is certainly deserving of our respect. One suspects that the rather sneering attitude towards the poem which has become popular during the last decade or so in Wales has as much to do with a contempt for our Christian past and a widespread rejection of the values of the gospel as it has with the intrinsic merit of the poem itself. From the time of his conversion it was the graves of the faithful from the Age of the Saints onwards which, for Gwenallt, made Wales' history a living reality, while the eyes of faith would certainly affirm the Holy Spirit's continual presence in the ongoing life of its people. Only a cynic would claim otherwise.

The two other poems in this volume which share the same title are much more craggy and uncompromising. In both the nation is pictured in the most unflattering terms, as a harlot:

> Though you are undeserving of our love,
> You, the base harlot of the street with servile voice,

and as a derelict. Yet the ideal, in both, is overtly Christian. It is because of her sinfulness that she has fallen, yet it is that very sinfulness which excites God's mercy and holds out the hope of redemption:

Have pity on her, merciful Father,
In your strength raise her up, then we shall clothe her
Body in all its glory.

The same is true of the final poem which is even harsher
than its predecessor:

Why have you given us this sorrow,
And pain like lead on flesh and blood?
Your language like a burden on our shoulders,
And your traditions fetters on our feet?
The cancer is shrivelling your whole countenance
    and form,
There are abscesses and scabs on your soul,
You are nothing but a nightmare in your own
    land,
And your survival is but a witch's dream.
And yet, we cannot leave you in the dirt
To the mockery and derision of this generation,
Your freedom of old is a ready sword to hand,
And your dignity is a shield to our breast,
So we take hold of our spears and spur on our
    horses
Lest we bring shame on our forefathers in their
    graves.

This is the Wales which is described in two other major
poems in the collection which deal with contemporary
themes, 'Ar Gyfeiliorn' or 'Astray' which I have already
mentioned, and the apocalyptic 'Y Gristionogaeth' ('Christianity'). Whereas both were typical of so much verse of
the 1930s, especially that of Auden, Spender and MacNeice
and their consciousness of the breakdown of civilization
and the coming of the dictators, yet each was highly
localized and specifically Christian in tone. Here the general crisis of European culture is particularized in the fate
of a single community, namely that of Wales which is itself

a combination of tradition and modernity. It is industrial Wales, highly mechanized yet blighted by unemployment and in political turmoil, which is both the scene of human drama and the object of the divine pity. Yet this same Wales is the inheritor of an ancient but living tradition of faith and communitarianism which adds depth and richness to its life and an added poignancy to its possible fate. In another feature characteristic of the 1930s, Gwenallt sees the political and religious situation in terms of stark antitheses rather than nuanced ambiguities:

> Has not your hour arrived, O God, your awesome
>   hour?
> Is not this, today – our age, our life – the fulness of
>   time?
> Anti-Christ's grievous hour in all its boldness, the
>   hour of challenge, perversity, death,
> The hour of vinegar and the tomb, the scorched hour
>   of the torch and the stake.

> 'Y Gristionogaeth' ('Christianity')

Just as the picture of Wales is hardly idealized, there was nothing comfortable or pietistic in the account of the situation in which the poet found himself. Yet within this situation Christianity remained a relevant factor, not only in so far as it possessed a philosophy of life which was sufficiently tough to meet the intellectual challenge and deep enough to encompass human needs, but also in that it still remained a popular faith option for a not insignificant portion of ordinary people. And it was this which did not allow Gwenallt – even during his Anglican phase – to depreciate the chapel culture of his day. The one poem which expresses this above all else and one of the best sonnets in *Ysgubau'r Awen* is the superb 'Sir Forgannwg' ('Glamorganshire'):

How empty are your colliers in their working clothes
With a mask of coaldust on their faces,
Paper currency in the vast exchange,
Exports from the docks of the world's greed:
In the rebellion of flesh and blood they raised
Pick and shovel to strike the god of their age,
But they were pinned down more firmly, hands and
    feet,
And more cement was laid at the base of their cross.
Sunday, however, sees them in clean attire,
In their faces shines the light of a living soul,
And in their sanctuary their song is heard,
The joyful hymns of God's royal race;
The cage is wound from the pit's depths to heaven
By the steel ropes of God's sure and ancient wheels.

This sonnet typifies Gwenallt's style: first an octave which
sets out in realistic detail the bleakness in which the people,
his people, find themselves, describing their situation and
plight, followed by six lines in which those same people
are transfigured and humanized by their faith, the final
couplet containing an apt and highly striking metaphorical
climax. Even in translation, this inventive and forceful use
of metaphor expresses the poem's feel even if the intricacies
of rhythm and rhyme are unfortunately lost. Yet what is
especially imposing about *Ysgubau'r Awen*, which contains less free verse than Gwenallt's subsequent volumes,
is its peculiarly effective combination of poetic style and
thematic substance.

II

'When a man is past fifty . . .'

In turning to his third volume of verse, *Eples* (*Ferment*)
(1951) – the pamphlet *Cnoi Cil*, which was very much in
the same vein as *Ysgubau'r Awen*, appeared in 1942 – we
find that the poet has, in the main, mellowed (though the
passion is still there waiting to erupt) and that the earlier
antitheses had yielded if not to synthesis at least to an
integration of sorts. There is still starkness, violence and
abruptness but also a meditative quality and, in places,
tranquillity as well. The first half-dozen poems were at one
time regarded not only as Gwenallt's finest but among the
best examples of verse which Wales produced during the
twentieth century. The nine four-line verses of 'Y Meirwon'
('The Dead') contain some of the poet's most memorable
visualizations and wordcraft and for a while they proved
to be sufficiently potent to establish a whole generation's
self-perception (see *Translations*, no. 26 p. 135). By any
measure this was poetry of tremendous power in which the
middle-aged poet looks back both in anger and resignation,
standing both apart from and in solidarity with the community of his youth. The depths of feeling tapped here
are deep indeed and intensified by the author's switching
indiscriminately from describing others – his childhood
contemporaries, the neighbouring family from Merthyr
Tydfil nicknamed 'The Martyrs' whose hollow cough was
blighted by tuberculosis, the pale coffined corpses and the
mute, courageous widows 'carrying coal, cutting firewood
and doing the garden/ Reading more often the story of the
suffering on the Cross' – to expressing his own emotions,
both memories of his hot-blooded, revolutionary youth
and his current reflections as a grown man. The use of

metaphor is as strong as ever, the steel cables binding him to his industrial past, death like a sleek, lethal leopard springing out to destroy its unsuspecting prey or like the echo of a warder doing his rounds (as a teenager during the Great War Gwenallt had spent two years in prison as a conscientious objector), and his turn of phrase is stunning: lungs being spewed into a bucket, 'charcoaled flesh . . . and a voice of ash', death underground or, as happened to his own father, death by being scalded by molten metal from a ladle, envisioned here as 'the hootered death; the dusty, choking, drunk death'. Imagery such as this was quite incomparable. The line in the penultimate stanza in which he describes the flowers with which those widows, on Palm Sunday, would dress their dead menfolk's graves, 'silicotic roses and lilies as white as gas', is surely exquisite and among the most memorable in modern Welsh literature. Yet for all the strong feeling which these memories excite, there is a composure, a coming to terms not with injustice but with human rightness and the dignity of those whose lives had been perfected by suffering:

Utopia vanished from the top of Gellionnen,
　　Abstract humanity, the classless, borderless world;
Today all that remains at the back of the memory
　　Is family and neighbourhood, the sacrifice and
　　　　suffering of man.

The theological theme, though understated, is patent. Utopia was the secular ideal of an equitable society achieved through human striving apart from divine grace. Its presupposition was man's innate goodness and capacity for perfection. It was a myth, but unlike the Christian myth of creation, fall and redemption, it could never square with reality because it rejected the fact of human depravity. This was Eden without the snake and as such it was intrinsically false. The strength of the Christian story lay in a realism drawn from revealed truth and it was through the dignity of their faith that the working-class communities of the South Wales valleys overcame their adversity.

Among the clutch of opening poems in *Eples* were 'Y Dirwasgiad' ('The Depression'), 'Cymdogion' ('Neighbours'), 'Colomennod' ('Doves') where the racing pigeons of the industrial workers represent the humanizing effect of an innocent pastime while also being symbolic of the regenerative ministry of the Holy Spirit. 'Morgannwg' ('Glamorgan') is a splendidly evocative description of the industrial South during early and mid-century in which religion, far from being an opiate of the people, is a normal, healthy aspect of their everyday lives. Although 'In the automated, proletarian villages' where the gantries whirled and the crane rolled along hardship and suffering were inevitable, yet human values flourished in the small things: workers keeping pigs or tending their gardens after a shift or singing '"All men, all things" and "Worthy is the Lamb"' in the local choir. Within those close yet modern communities, industrialized certainly but still betraying their rural roots, both ideology and irreligion would be undermined by adversity which in turn bred solidarity and sympathy among all:

> The hooter would quench the flash of humour
> And silence unbelief and Socialism too:
> The funeral cortèges would wind quietly and dim
> Between the clanging of the steelworks and tinmills:
> At the power of the hymn the whitegowned dead
> Would rise from their graves and move beyond the
>   stacks.

This was a Stanley Spencer vision of the resurrection but altogether tougher, more serious; eternal rest beckoned beyond the smoking chimneys and the grime, yet the great hymns of faith sung with such gusto even – especially – at funeral services would not only fortify those who were left behind but would express faith in Christ's ultimate conquest over death.

Along with 'Sul y Fferm' ('The Farm's Sunday'), the two remaining major poems at the beginning of *Eples* are 'Rhydcymerau' and 'Sir Forgannwg a Sir Gaerfyrddin' ('Glamorganshire and Carmarthenshire'). The poem dedicated to Rhydcymerau, the Carmarthenshire village from which Gwenallt's parents had moved late in the nineteenth century in order to find work, is not typical. It was a prose poem whereas most of his work to date had been in the strict metres, sonnets or rhymed stanzas at the very least. But here the poet seeks to describe a lost reality bleakly, unencumbered by metrical pattern. It is a poem of such importance that we give it again, in a different translation from that provided by Patrick Thomas:

They have planted the saplings for the third world war
On the land of Esgeir-ceir and the fields of Tir-bach
Near Rhydcymerau.

I remember my grandmother in Esgeir-ceir
Sitting by the fire pleating her apron;
Her face was as yellow and wrinkled as a medieval manuscript,
And the Welsh on her aged lips the Welsh of Pantycelyn.
She was a piece of last century's Puritan Wales.
My grandfather, though I never met him,
Was a 'character'; a brisk, twinkling little creature,
Fond of his pint;
He had strayed in from the eighteenth century.
They raised nine children,
Poets, deacons and Sunday School teachers,
Each a leader in his small locality.

My Uncle Dafydd used to farm Tir-bach,
A country poet and local rhymester,
His song to the cockerel was famous in those parts:
>'The little cock goes scratching
>In the garden here and there'.
It was to him that I would go during my summer
holidays
To help tend the sheep and fashion lines of
cynghanedd,
Englynion and eight-line stanzas in the eight-seven
measure.
He too raised eight children,
The eldest was a Calvinistic Methodist minister
Who also wrote verse.
Our family was full of poets.

And by now there is nothing left but trees,
Their impertinent roots sucking the old soil dry:
Trees where there was once community,
A forest where there were once farms,
Bastardized South Wales English where there was
once poetry and divinity,
The barking of foxes where there had once been the
cries of children and of lambs.
And there, in its dark midst,
The lair of the English Minotaur;
And on trees, as though on crosses,
The skeletons of poets, elders, ministers and Sunday
School teachers
Being bleached by the sun,
And washed by the rain and licked dry by the wind.

The poem is harsh, brutal but exceedingly memorable. It
is a protest against the barbarity of capitalism and the
expendability of tradition and all that is civilized and
humane. For Gwenallt it was a parable of twentieth-
century Wales. Yet for all its savagery – and savagery did

not, in the main, characterize *Eples* – it belonged to a wider vision in which the splendours of the past could in fact be preserved in order to become part of a contemporary synthesis, a vision in which the rural ideal was compatible with both modernity and faith. The symbol of that modernity, for the poet, was Glamorganshire, the community which had spearheaded Britain's industrial revolution and for all its suffering and turmoil remained culturally rich and socially vibrant. Despite the early influence of Marxism and the continuing presence of religious apathy within its borders, industrialization there did not conform to the English or continental stereotype by indicating secularity. Well into the twentieth century, religion, especially in its Nonconformist guise, remained an important social phenomenon in South Wales.

Although the industrial heartland was much wider than Glamorgan and included the more Anglicized Monmouthshire in the east, and east Carmarthenshire in the west as well, Glamorganshire remained Gwenallt's shorthand for industrial Wales. Glamorganshire and Carmarthenshire together stand for the two sides of a single picture, Carmarthenshire being symbolic of the older, rural ideal. In 'Glamorganshire and Carmarthenshire' (*Translations* no. 23 p. 130) he begins by describing the village of Talyllychau or Talley, situated in the lush Carmarthenshire hills between Llandeilo and Lampeter, which was both the site of a beautiful and ruined Cistercian abbey and the home of Thomas Lewis, an excellent eighteenth-century hymnist who worked as the local blacksmith. Williams of Pantycelyn, of course, was an even greater hymn writer than Thomas Lewis, in fact Wales' greatest ever, and like Lewis a native of Carmarthenshire. Llansadwrn was the parish in which Rhydcymerau was situated. Caeo, another of the county's parishes, was also renowned for its eighteenth-century hymnwriters while Crug-y-bar, a small village near Talley, had given its name to one of the best-loved and most popular hymn tunes of Gwenallt's day. The poem, therefore, is full of references to popular Nonconformity and the Welsh religious past. Yet the poem derives its potency from the tension and antithesis, never wholly resolved, between this idealized, spiritual past and its evocation of the political present. (Though even here the poet is referring to his youth rather than to the South Wales of 1951.) The soapbox in Pontardawe's town square, the incessant noise of the steelworks and its cranes, the political agitation for social justice and a living wage belong to the period before the Great War, as do William Abraham or 'Mabon', the Victorian miners' leader and Keir Hardie, founder of the Independent Labour Party and the man who would ultimately embody the aspirations of the new South Wales. All are conjured up, and such is their influence that they all but obliterate the religious past. All but, but not quite. And by the final stanza we have Gwenallt's preferred accommodation between all that is just and honest in the one with all that is good, civilized and humane in the other. The span of the cross and the inclusiveness of Christ's Church are things far greater than either an unworldly puritanism or a this-worldly socialism, both of which tend to become mere ideologies, the one religious, the other secular. It is this poem, more than any other, which characterizes Gwenallt's mature view of Wales in which he attempts a reconciliation between rural and urban, religious and humanist, ancient and contemporary, and achieves it not by the dilution of conviction but by a complex mutual enrichment.

During recent years each of these poems has been strongly criticized and, in some cases, their underlying philosophy has been pilloried. In what has been a remarkable *volte-face*, notably *Eples* but Gwenallt's verse generally has been removed from the pantheon and summarily dismissed. 'The Dead', for instance, has been deconstructed so as to reveal a plethora of inconsistencies which reveal psychological guilt on the poet's part for having turned his back on both his community and his social class. It was all too easy, according to his detractors, to be converted to a pliant and intrinsically reactionary Christianity and thus to contract out of the need for revolutionary political change. Rather than painting a true picture of his times, sentimental myopia blinded Gwenallt to the social and psychological realities of his day. 'Glamorganshire and Carmarthenshire' has also been taken to task for succumbing to gross oversimplification, its ideological superficiality being hidden by rhetorical sleight of hand. Each stanza, it has been said, contains an obvious contradiction, but such is the strength of the poem's rhetoric and metaphor – the blacksmith-hymnist fashioning his hymn like a horseshoe on his anvil, reinforced by the poem's metrical beat, is acknowledged as being quite brilliant – that the reader is deceived into accepting the poet's worldview at face value. On closer analysis, the synthesis which the poet claimed to have achieved was a chimera, it never existed.[5]

The most persistent attack on Gwenallt's Christian vision has come from Professor John Rowlands, perhaps the most influential of contemporary Welsh-language critics, and he finds it distasteful in the extreme. The obsession with sin he finds unwholesome and the idea of human (and Welsh) corruption coming under divine judgement fills him with horror. Gwenallt, he claims, used his profuse gifts of imagination in a fundamentally warped and pernicious cause and what is more, for a long time he managed to take many along with him. One of the great benefits of a post-Christian and now almost totally secular culture, he implies, is to have saved Welsh literature from the malign clutches of this diminutive bard.[6] For a younger generation of critics much affected by Professor Rowlands' opinions, this has become a virtual dogma.

It seems to me that none of these criticisms are insuperable and that the memorable quality of Gwenallt's verse will persist. The deconstructionalist critique is the most tendentious, and although (to be fair) it has been delivered in a benign spirit, it remains contrived and unconvincing. Even the censure that the poet has failed to achieve an integrated vision – made, by the way, by a critic (Robert Rhys) whose own Christian commitment is unassailable – appears quite simply to be wrong. Secularists may find it jarring but there will be no doubt about Christianity's ability to cope with the challenge of the twenty-first century or to continue to say something important about the human condition generally, and it is because of this that Gwenallt's verse will still be read with profit by whoever finds the transcendent realities in which he or she believes satisfying. The remainder of this essay will attempt to analyze the specifically religious convictions which come to the fore in some of the lesser-known poems in *Eples* and in Gwenallt's later verse from *Gwreiddiau* (*Roots*) (1959) and the posthumous *Y Coed* (*The Trees*) (1969).

III

The prophet of Europe's ruins

The theme of sinfulness, so fully worked out in the early collection, is evident again in *Eples* (as is the related subject of flesh and spirit) though now it is attached much more soundly to the fate of Europe during its recent past and its still uncertain future. If *Ysgubau'r Awen* and *Cnoi Cil* had been published under the shadow of the Second World War when few knew what its outcome would be, the author of *Eples* had been made all too familiar with the horrors of Hiroshima, Nagasaki and the Holocaust and was currently experiencing the chill winds of the Cold War. Sinfulness, for the poet, has less to do with the bourgeois mores of conventional morality than with a radical human perversion which manifested itself as much in the social and political sphere as in the realm of the individual. The gypsy fortune-teller in her fairground caravan, for all her innocent exoticism, is symbolic of those dark powers which, from the days of Samuel, Saul and the Witch of Endor, have mesmerized humankind, drawing out its capacity for evil. The tragedy of the twentieth century was that barbarism and the demonic, far from having withered away with technological advance, were as potent in Hitler's Germany and elsewhere as in the Old Testament Book of Samuel ('Y Sipsi' ('The Gypsy')). Biblical allusions are employed again in Gwenallt's reflection on humankind whose Tower of Babel reaching the heavens is an enclosed structure, doorless and windowless, its technologically advanced but morally stunted inhabitants oblivious of the glory of the stars above and unconscious of the rich depths below ('Dyn' ('Mankind')). As with the earlier poems, certain animals become symbolic of human pride and iniquity just as others – the doves especially – are made to express hope and redemption. A hedgehog, spotted one day on a journey from Gwenallt's home to nearby Nanteos, a place sanctified in Welsh legend as the resting place of the Holy Grail and during the medieval centuries a place of pilgrimage, becomes the symbol for humankind's perpetual rejection of God. The picture of the creature – putrid, spherical and thorny – is brutal and typically twentieth-century:

> He is the prophet on Europe's ruins
> Archetype of her letters and fine arts;
> It is he who filled the void where once was the Trinity
> O! eternal orb. O! thorn-laden deity.

'Y Draenog' ('The Hedgehog')

The use of the psychoanalytical term 'archetype' is quite deliberate as is the allusion to Christ's crown of thorns in the description of the creatures' spikes. If this admittedly brutal poem has been heavily criticized for its extreme and unflattering portrayal of human corruption, there is also evidence in *Eples* of a gentler, less judgmental strain where human imperfection is met by the divine pity leading to salvation and wholeness. This is exemplified by the interesting poem to the so-called 'fatling' of Isaiah's prophecy: 'The wolf also shall dwell with the lamb and the leopard shall lie down with the kid, and the calf with the young lion and the fatling together, and a little child shall lead them' (Isa. 11:6).

Never once did I see him
Nor do I know what he looked like,
Was he black, grey or red,
What, Isaiah, was his background and pedigree?
This fatling.

He stalked through the centuries to his dire lair
In Siberia, Belsen and Buchenwald,
And above the trees of Hiroshima
He left his slimy trail,
That fatling.

Were that creature to glimpse His glory
At the Cross which binds together earth and heaven,
In the company of the cow and the ox and the lamb,
He, too, would graze his lush grass;
The fatling.

'Yr Anifail Bras' ('The Fatling')

There are other poems in the same vein which, although they have drawn little attention in the past, are nevertheless thought-provoking and stimulating. In 'Yr Eryrod' ('The Eagles'), he visualizes those formidable birds first as God's saints soaring down from the skies and after alighting on the earth being transformed into wholly unprepossessing creatures walking *incognito* among its inhabitants yet doing God's strange work: 'Giving up all to the poor, a coat to a tramp/ And kissing a leper's cheek'. Then in a striking change of metaphor, he describes the saints' lasting effect upon their generation:

> Like businessmen they erected temples to God
> And bore the stigmata of Christ into the hands of
> their time.

The eagle, of course, is symbolic not only of the saints but of other aspects of the Christian tradition. As a faithful and communicant member of the Church in Wales, Gwenallt would listen week by week to the Scriptures being read from the huge brass eagle-shaped lectern in Llanbadarn parish church. The eagle was also the symbol of John's Gospel, the one New Testament book above all others which emphasizes the fact of God's incarnation in Christ. Having been redeemed from metaphysical speculation of a Platonist kind by a Christianity which takes time, place and human history seriously, the poet found that the very words of the gospel underlined the essence of his faith in all its concrete particularity:

> John the Evangelist; the king of the eagles
> It was he who raised me above the insubstantial
> shadows;
> His Welsh felled me with a hammer-blow
> And cleared away the romantic undergrowth with the
> scythe of his words.

He mentions too 'Apostolic eagles; my theological eagles,/ Staring at the Logos in eternity,/ Who strode from the goal of the far Trinity/ To clothe Himself in flesh . . .', and the 'eucharistic eagles' who presided over that transformation of the elements in the bread and wine which vouchsafed Christ's real presence within his creation.

That other bird which features so poignantly in the Christian story is the cockerel, the symbol not of St John but of St Peter and his betrayal of Christ. In a marvellously evocative poem entitled 'The Weathercock' ('Y Ceiliog Gwynt'), Gwenallt pictures Peter's cockerel having found a place not so much in the church but ever present above it, on its spires, still ready to turn in the prevailing wind.

> By now you too are part of the Church
> Having been raised up from your perch to its tower;
> > You were given a place in His scheme
> > When you crowed twice on that night
> And turned an old apostle's heart to water.

Despite its fickleness, the cockerel's place is secure. The betrayal of Christ, far from being the cause of the apostle's perdition, led in fact to conviction, costly repentance and an assurance of forgiveness through the divine mercy. This leads, in turn, to the poet's prayer: 'O Wind, give again his old gift/ To raise, as from the heart of hasty Peter,/ The violet tears to the eyes of the world'. Brief as it is, there is no doubt that this is one of Gwenallt's finest and most heartfelt religious poems.

Apart from these poems in which animals, especially birds, symbolize spiritual realities, there are others in *Eples* which relate directly to the Christian verities. In 'Cymun yr Arglwyddes' ('The Lady's Communion') the Blessed Virgin is portrayed as the lady of the house who, having laid on a sumptuous harvest supper for her workers, serves them with the wine herself (*Translations*, no. 2 p. 95). 'The Two Eves' ('Y Ddwy Efa') is a simple lyric in which the Church, spotless in her purity, is pictured as having been taken from Christ's pierced side in order to redeem mankind just as Eve, according to the Genesis narrative, had been taken from Adam's ribs. 'Cwm yr Eglwys', the spot in Pembrokeshire where only one wall remains of a church which has long been washed away into Cardigan Bay, illustrates the Church's persistent presence despite the destructive power of secularity. Here the poet intertwines his call to rebuild the Church with the old Welsh legend of Cantre'r Gwaelod, the lost commote in the Irish Sea which was deluged due to the all-too-human foolishness of its guardians, while another poem in this set is a meditation on a biblical event. In his chapter Donald Allchin states that he is not surprised to find Gwenallt referring, in his autobiographical essay, to the gospel story of the transfiguration. The poem 'Yr Eglwys' ('The Church', *Translations* no. 24 p. 132) not only alludes to Christ's experience on the mountain when the heavenly glory manifested itself so strongly, but it expresses all of Gwenallt's central experiences and convictions in a very marked way.

> The Church is tents pitched on the side of the Mount
>   of Transfiguration,
>   Tents where Peter wanted his tents to be,
> On the Mountain where Christ shone like the sun on
>   the snow,
>   Without the snow cooling the sun and without
>   the sun melting the snow.
>
> We were once in the valley thundering from our
>   soapboxes
>   Against the workers' Egypt and the bosses'
>   strawless bricks,
> Asking Engels and Karl Marx, instead of Christ on
>   the Mountain,
>   To lead us to the Communist Canaan at the
>   journey's end.

The three verses which follow describe the poet's intellectual pilgrimage; his early faith in scientific advancement and his erstwhile acceptance of Hegel's Idealist, a-historical philosophy which envisioned Christ as a fleshless abstraction, 'a part of the crib-less, grave-less, colourless

Absolute'. Yet harsh experience gave the lie to such optimism; his need was for something more than 'The wooly Absolute who could not walk through sin and the depths of being'. A scientific and materialist vision of the world which was blind to any sense of transcendent glory, deprived men and women of what they needed most, a satisfying creed to live by. It was this that the gospel of incarnation purported to provide:

> When the Spirit thins the canvas we shall see that the
> > universe is a creation,
> > That the worker is a person because he is the
> > child of God,
> And see Christ rising up from his Cross and Grave
> > like the glory
> > Of the sun in the wounded snow to give light to
> > the seventh Heaven.

Perhaps the most arresting work in this sequence is the poem 'Cip' ('A Glimpse') in which Gwenallt reflects on the nature of permanence and change. Considering in turn the different philosophical schemes such as Darwinism, Einstein's relativity theory, materialism and the like, he realizes that behind all change, signified by the sight of generations of students coming into his classes at the University of Wales, Aberystwyth, and then leaving again with the regularity of the sea's ebb and flow, there is one face which underlies all others; it is the face of the ascended and transcendent Christ. Yet although comforting in its permanence, there is something unnerving about the divine presence:

> I wish, at times, to catch a glimpse, one glimpse, of
> > that face
> But I tremble if in case like Icarus of old
> I do so and plummet like an arrow into the sea,
> His plumes scattered and blown away by the wind.

'It is a fearful thing to fall into the hands of the living God' (Heb. 10:31).

Eples includes other subjects apart from the religious: there are poems in the praise tradition including what must be one of the finest of all more recent *cywyddau* to the bard's erstwhile teacher and mentor, T. Gwynn Jones; there are poems on Celtic themes and those on Wales including 'Dewi Sant' ('St David'), which has been referred to in the previous essay. It is difficult, though, to differentiate between these diverse strata as the underlying philosophy is so unified and strong. In the end all things begin with God and refer back to Him not as an abstraction but as the God who, in Christ, has reconciled the world to himself. It was St David who, according to the poet,

> . . . spoke to us about God's natural Order,
> The person, the family, the nation and the society of
> nations,
> And the Cross keeping us from turning one of them
> into a god.

This is perhaps as good a précis as any of Gwenallt's mature life-view.

IV

Carrying Calvary to the midst of the works

Although the poet's fourth volume of verse entitled *Gwreiddiau* (*Roots*) is said to have made clear how his muse had stagnated – it was nothing short of fundamentalist propaganda according to my late esteemed Professor of Welsh, Bedwyr Lewis Jones! – nevertheless this 1959 collection contains more than a few striking and moving pieces; some more recent critical appraisals of the work have been surprisingly positive as to its quality and abiding value. The theological content of the book permeates the whole, in fact this was the most obviously religious of Gwenallt's work to date. The poet is unashamedly Christian, indeed more than one of the poems refers back to his conversion a generation or more earlier and shows how his spiritual development had subsequently progressed. 'Yr Hen Emynau' ('The Old Hymns') is a case in point (see *Translations*, no. 8 p. 108).

The Nonconformist spirituality in which Gwenallt was brought up had been moulded by its hymns. More even than preaching and infinitely more than any formal sacramental teaching, it was through the content and the singing of their hymns – Williams Pantycelyn, Ann Griffiths, Thomas Lewis and the rest – that chapel folk would be introduced to spiritual experience and nurtured in the faith. The unconscious effect of these hymns in the context of popular communal worship at a receptive age was seldom less than profound – as any visit to an international match at Cardiff Arms Park up to the 1970s would have shown! Yet for Gwenallt their influence, albeit unconsciously, was considerably more than cultural. It was through them that God's presence had perpetuated itself in his soul. During his agnostic, unbelieving phase, the poet's contempt for Christianity, Nonconformity particularly, was withering, yet the experience which the poem expresses, so reminiscent of Francis Thompson being unwillingly pursued by his 'Hound of Heaven' or C. S. Lewis being followed, cornered and ultimately overcome by the God whom he had absolutely no desire to meet, is powerfully captured. Here spiritual experience, theological conviction, poetic sensibility and the dreadful consciousness of God's holiness meet; the context, as it was in *Ysgubau'r Awen*, is the history of industrial South Wales. This poem is characteristic of the volume throughout.

A second piece entitled 'Y Dewis' ('The Choice')

expresses not only the existential drama of an intelligent and literate adult's religious conversion but gives a wry insight into much twentieth-century intellectual history as well. Patrick Thomas's translation, contained in the next section of this book, captures its nuances perfectly. Far from taking the believer away from the world, the Christian redemption which the poet experiences is the very thing which takes him into the midst of the fray. Although this should be an obvious and incontrovertible inference from the incarnational principle of the gospel, this deduction has not always been made: in many cases Christianity has been interpreted in pietist fashion by Nonconformists and Anglicans alike. But for Gwenallt there could be no contracting out of one's secular responsibility and it was the dogmas of orthodox Christianity which made this fact plain. Neither secular humanism nor a bloodless theological liberalism had the wherewithal to send him into the human arena. The point is made in a third and equally arresting autobiographical poem 'Gwlad ac Ynys' ('Land and Island') in which he recalls his youthful rejection of an outmoded and superstitious creed in favour of the religion of progress. In the cultured land of modernity all was ordered and rational there being neither sin nor tragedy beneath its tilled soil:

> The old superstitions – the virgin birth,
> Miracles, God becoming man,
> God dying on a cross and rising from his tomb –
> Were thrown like refuse into the dustbins
> And emptied onto the tips to be burned.

Darwin, Huxley, Bradlaugh, McCabe, the *Golden Bough* and the rest, all of which had been staple fare for the poet as a young man, had woven their magic and made the old beliefs redundant. But what had drawn him back to the convictions of his forefathers was not, curiously, antiquarianism but modernity itself, the experience of life in all its twentieth-century complexity which had convinced him that the tilled soil of rationality was merely a covering for more primitive lusts, evils and neuroses which the theologians, true doctors of the soul, had long understood:

And beyond the horizon the crimson Christ
Like the unseen sun, as Pascal and Kierkegaard had
    said,
Cast His true, redemptive, wholesome and fruitful
    light
Upon the land's poor, guilty acres . . .

That poor, guilty land, of course, was Wales. Not only had the gospel taken him from the realm of the theoretical to that of the concrete, it had particularized the universal, as we see in the fine poem to Bishop William Morgan in *Gwreiddiau* and the earlier poem entitled 'Dewi Sant' ('St David') in *Eples* which have been considered in the previous chapter.

His poems about Wales, 'Y Genedl' ('The Nation') and 'Cymru', his fifth published under the same title, are less derogatory than some of his earlier ones though they follow roughly the same theme – Wales personified as the harlot or the unfaithful partner. But now the tone has changed and harshness has been replaced by sympathy. In 'The Nation' the central metaphor is that of the invalid:

It is not our wish to bend over you in your illness
Like infallibly healthy doctors,
Applying our stethoscope to your breast and our
    fingers to your pulse
And examining your hopeless condition and your
    scabs.
As we try to diagnose from the symptoms the nature
    of your disease
We feel the fever of it in our own heads.

What we want to do is to take you to the hospital
   ward
Where man is stripped down to his sheer naked-
   ness;
Where the world and its pomp, money and position,
Comfort and the things of the flesh have to be left
   without:
One has nothing there but a cupboard, a pot and
   pangs of pain
In the monastery next door to death:

We want to take you on a trolley to the operating
   theatre,
To the room of the sterilized scissors and scalpels,
In whose light and silence throughout the centuries
The saints' chronic cancer of guilt has been excised:
The white-robed Surgeon is performing his horrid
   operation
In the merciful, life-restoring theatre of his passion.

Along with a collection of epigrams commenting, often
pungently and sometimes unfairly, on the foibles of mid-
twentieth-century life and a long narrative poem which
uses the biblical story of the Prophet Elijah's altercation
with Jezebel from 1 Kings 16–21 in allegorical fashion to
comment on the fate of the Christian civilization of Europe,
Gwreiddiau concludes with a handful of poems which
explore doctrinal themes and celebrate the seasons and
feasts of the Church. One would not expect the evangelical
and Protestant doctrine of penal substitution to yield itself
readily to an artistic treatment but in the poem 'Barabbas',
a portrait of the New Testament character whose life was
spared in exchange for Christ's, this is what it gets. His
sonnet entitled 'Duw' ('God') is as blatantly theological as
any poem could dare be, but the artistry is not altogether
lost in theory and speculation:

He is no yogi, no rule-of-silence hermit
Contemplating His own great navel;
Nor is He a mathematician wrapped in the mist of
    heaven
Solving man's transcendental problems:
He did not create our world like a pure artist,
Dandyish, self-centred, skilfully scheming;
Nor did He set it moving along steel rails
After His scientific hand had raised a head of steam.
He is who He is; with love beneath his breast
As though seething amongst all His thoughts,
And this love casts up wave after wave
Of passion to beat against the grizzled shores of our
    world;
And the ninth wave broke on Calvary,
Bearing on its foam the vessel of our deliverance.

This and other poems as well – 'Amser' ('Time'), 'Y Grawys' ('Lent'), 'Corff Crist' ('The Body of Christ' – quoted, in full, by Donald Allchin in his chapter) and 'Nadolig 1955' ('Christmas 1955') to select a few at random – all repay close reading and contribute towards as accomplished a treatment of Christian faith as made by any major twentieth-century poet.

V

The Catholicity of the Word

By 1959, when this volume was published, the poet was sixty years old, his convictions having been long established and his reputation within his own country secure. His muse was still, on the whole, catholic although he had left the Church in Wales and returned to the Calvinistic

Methodism of his childhood and youth. The biblical and theological renaissance of the mid-1930s to the 50s linked to such Protestant thinkers as Barth, Brunner, Niebuhr and their disciples had convinced Gwenallt that, far from undermining catholic truth, the Reformation had rediscovered much of the richness of the early Church's faith. If informed by patristic learning and sacramental wholeness, Protestantism was a valid interpretation of apostolic Christianity. It also laid store on evangelical experience, the *experience* of the saved soul, which came to take a more central place in Gwenallt's thinking the older he became. If the Anglican Church in Wales during the late 1950s was not at its most propitious, Welsh evangelicalism was undergoing something of a spiritual and intellectual renewal with which Gwenallt was happy to align himself.[7] Much of this is expressed in his final volume of verse, *Y Coed* (*The Trees*) published posthumously in 1969. Although many of the fifty or so poems incorporated here would, no doubt, have been polished and emended had the author lived, they include some of his finest. Some thirty were written following a visit to the Holy Land and describe biblical incidents in the light of this journey. They are, on the whole, graphic and arresting: it is obvious that this pilgrimage affected him deeply. Then there are the familiar themes of Wales, modernity, Europe and her civilization as well as epigrammatic verses and some touching eulogies to his friends. His grand poem 'Sir Gaerfyrddin' ('Carmarthenshire') presented to Gwynfor Evans, the Plaid Cymru MP, on having been elected in 1966 to represent that constituency in Westminster, is the last of a series on the familiar rural theme. More prose than poetry, it lists in quick succession those people and places who had made that county so important in Welsh history. Idris Foster, in a most perceptive review, likened it to a bidding prayer in which the benefactors of the past are evoked and praised.

Among the explicitly religious poems 'Swper yr Arglwydd' ('The Lord's Supper') and 'Catholigrwydd'

('Catholicity') are especially noteworthy; both have been translated by Patrick Thomas and are included in the next section. In the first of these he describes what seems to have been a specific spiritual experience which occurred during a service of Holy Communion in Llanbadarn parish church. It was a dark day, damp and cold, hardly propitious circumstances in which to be granted a vision of God. In the quiet, cavernous church everything seemed so far away: the altar, the distant cross and the chancel, and then, while partaking of the eucharist, the poet was given an insight into the miracle of incarnation; Bethlehem, he says, with its angels and shepherds and animals, descended from on high and he saw Mary wrapping up God's infinity in a napkin and rocking eternity to sleep in his cradle. The birth of Christ was all of a piece with his life lived in perfect obedience to the Father and offered up on humanity's behalf, a sacrifice which transformed life in its entirety. The sound of the rain outside, reminiscent of the running water which the poet had once heard in an Italian city square, was symbolic of the Holy Spirit's gentle, healing presence while a shaft of light lit up the cross and enveloped the altar in the fire of Christ's divine humanity. Outside the whole of creation, the trees and the rivers and the sea, blazed with God's glory.

In 'Catholicity' the poet returns to a subject which had fascinated him all his Christian life, that of flesh, spirit and their transfiguration in order to serve God's purpose in the world: he also returns to the person of Christ 'imprisoned by his flesh and his Jewish bones/ Within the confines of his land'. This was the Christ who gave himself as a living sacrifice to the Father before being raised up anew in the miracle of resurrection. And the result?

> And since then Cardiff is as near as Calvary
> And Bangor every inch as Bethlehem,
> The storms are stilled on Cardigan Bay,
> And in every street the afflicted
> Find healing from the touch of his hem.

Flesh and spirit, the particular and the universal, the ordinary and the extraordinary are all harmonized in Christ, the incarnation of God's redemptive love.

Despite the remarkable quality of the poems quoted above, there are two particular poems which, although they have received little widespread attention, are among the most memorable that he ever wrote: I refer to the magnificent elegy to the Bangor theologian J. E. Daniel and an astounding poem entitled 'Trychineb Aber-fan' ('The Aberfan Disaster').

After gaining quite remarkable firsts in Mods, Greats and Theology in Jesus College, Oxford, John Edward Daniel had returned to Bangor as a tutor in Christian Doctrine in the university's Faculty of Theology. A local boy and Congregationalist son of the manse, he soon made his mark as a serious disciple of Karl Barth. By the mid-1930s he had come to personify the Calvinist renewal among a younger generation of Welsh ministers and theologians. Like Gwenallt he was pugnacious and that pugnacity as well as his intellectual genius is alluded to in the poem. As is his politics, for he became, very early on, a leading nationalist and member of *Plaid Genedlaethol Cymru*, the Welsh Nationalist Party. The poem, which is too long to quote in full, has an introduction, three constituent parts and a conclusion. This is how it begins:

> The mansion which he constructed had three great halls,
> But before building it, it was necessary to destroy the old.
> He procured his sledge-hammer from St Augustine
> In order to loosen Hawen and Schleiermacher's
>   unsound foundations,
> And shatter the modern Pelagians' soft walls.
> Calvin and Luther gave him his pickaxe
> With which to excavate surer foundations to put in
>   their place
> And raise upon them the walls of his strong, sturdy
>   building.

The strength of this introduction is in its references, its alliterative quality and its striking central metaphor. St Augustine, bishop of Hippo in North Africa and the greatest of all the Christian fathers of the West was pre-eminently the theologian of redemption and grace: the Celtic monk Pelagius – in Welsh 'Morgan' – was his opponent and antithesis who claimed that mankind had within itself the ability to reach perfection. 'Hawen' was the pen-name of the Revd David Adams, the precursor of theological liberalism in Wales, and F. D. E. Schleiermacher was the boldest and best of the German theologians of Romanticism and the Enlightenment. Calvin and Luther were the greatest among the Protestant Reformers. Metrically the fifth line is powerful indeed: '. . . *A dryllio muriau meddal y Morganiaid modern*' though its strength is lost, rather, in translation. Persons, places, names and connections became increasingly important in Gwenallt's later poems and are used here to considerable effect.

The first of the great halls in Daniel's mansion was the theological hall, the abode of the queen of the sciences:

On the walls of the upper room was the Apostles'
    Creed
The Nicene and the Athanasian Creed and the Te
    Deum;
And on the table by the window, in the light of the
    Holy Spirit,
Was the Bible and a volume of the works of
    Pantycelyn.
On the shelves were the volumes of the theologians of
    the centuries,
And on the uppermost shelf Evangelical theology from
    Tertullian
To Kierkegaard to Karl Barth . . .

'John Edward Daniel'

The renewal of orthodoxy which had occurred in some parts of the Church following the Great War is duly described as is its basis in God's working out the salvation of mankind through the incarnation, death and resurrection of Christ, his Son. It had been J. E. Daniel, more than anyone, who had made these themes his own and shared them with his compatriots and contemporaries in such a vivid and effective manner: 'He was this queen's ambassador in Wales;/ A minister of Jesus Christ; a crusader of St Paul.'

The second hall was given over to the classics, *litterae humaniores* and the glory of Europe's ancient past and the third was the hall of Wales; each is described, its contents listed and their significance made plain. The interconnectedness of these halls, which Gwenallt mentions in the concluding paragraph of the elegy, underlines the wholeness of Daniel's vision in which sound theology, a rootedness in Western civilization's classical past and a sincere love of Wales coalesce to produce a synthesis not unlike the poet's own: 'To bind the humanism of the Renaissance to the Trinitarian theology,/ And place the Church's doctrines at the heart of the crisis of Wales:/ To bind Jerusalem and Athens and Bangor.' Each received of Daniel's best, his razor-sharp intellect, his wide horizons, his infectious and guileless enthusiasm all of which are now gone in the road accident which took his life, '*y modur a'r mudandod*' – 'the motorcar and the silence' – the terseness of the original phrase, its alliteration and assonance, express the poignancy of the loss exquisitely. According to Idris Foster this poem is 'unquestionably to be counted among Gwenallt's greatest works'.[8]

The same must be said of the poem entitled 'The Aberfan Disaster'. At 9.15 on the morning of 21 October 1966 a coal-tip engulfed the junior school in the Glamorganshire village of Aberfan killing 116 children and 28 adults. The significance of such an appalling loss of life for the recent history of Wales was profound; it was through coal that industrial South Wales had established its identity and character but here fundamental questions about God, providence and the suffering of the innocent had to be faced. Like the Great War and the Holocaust, Aberfan was, in Wales, a defining moment in the way in which a whole generation viewed their existence. And it was Gwenallt, more than anyone, who looked the tragedy in the eye and out of the mute anguish of the creation provided comfort and some semblance of meaning.

Sparely though vividly the poem's four opening paragraphs describe the tragedy: the landslide, the junior school like a living dam and the eerie, solid silence which followed; the rescue and retrieval of the small bodies and their being washed and laid to rest in Bethania:

> Was there ever in a Welsh Chapel, in the sanctuary
>   and in the gallery,
> Such a strange congregation, and in its schoolroom
>   such silent pupils?

Following this the poet moves to the Holy Land and describes, with the same spare intensity, an aspect of the New Testament story. It was in Jerusalem, following the nativity, that Herod had killed the innocents and in Ramah that Rachel had shed tears for Benjamin, the dearest of her children, yet at least some reason could be gleaned from those ancient barbarities. No such comfort was forthcoming for the mothers of Aberfan. Theirs, he claims, were 'the twentieth century's most bitter tears'. The poem's fourth paragraph reflects on that history which Gwenallt had done so much to express and interpret, that of Glamorganshire and its heavy industry. South Wales had experienced tragedies before, its coal being red from the spilt blood of generations of men who had lost their lives underground. But this was different; these were children, the bearers of hope for a better future, a hope which had been crushed by the dead weight of man's greed.

When Jesus of Nazareth had returned with Mary and Joseph and escaped from Herod's clutches, he had grown and become a man, and in the fullness of time had been called upon, in Gethsemane, to drink the cup, 'the cup which was filled with man's wretchedness and God's wrath'. On the cross, crucified between two criminals, wearing his blood like a garment with his grief-stricken mother looking on, 'He too was forsaken by his Father in the three-hour darkness after the eclipse'. His was the horror of innocent, vicarious suffering and godforsakenness at its extreme: 'He plumbed to the depths which are deeper than the suffering of Aberfan, man's demonic depths and the eternal depths of God.' The only comfort which can be gleaned from such senseless, innocent suffering is that God himself is intimately involved in it, has taken it upon Himself and through that costly empathy can strengthen and console the bereaved and provide them with the assurance of redemption and resurrection.

> From his wounds
> And the blood of his brow flowed to us, sinners,
>   righteousness and pity,
> Forgiveness and love; and our hands strengthened by
>   grace we can clutch
> The bond which binds us to him; a bond that tragedy
>   will never break.

Before the advent of Moltmann's 'crucified God', Gwenallt's poem pointed to a theodicy which was true to the biblical revelation and spoke so powerfully to the bitterest experience of industrialized Wales. Of all his poems to the industrial South, this was the most solemn, the most memorable and perhaps the best. It marked a fitting close to an exceptional poetical career.

In the thirty years since Gwenallt's death, on 23 December 1968 at the age of sixty-nine, Wales, Europe and the world have changed inestimably. The renaissance of Welsh national consciousness (which the imagery of his poetry had done so much to establish) would only later register in the specific political and cultural gains of Welsh-medium education, a Welsh-language television channel and latterly a measure of devolution via the National Assembly. Yet the new Wales, although in some ways an improvement on the old, has lost much of its former character and glory. The rural ideal so memorably portrayed in the figure of Carmarthenshire has been all but destroyed by economic and demographic changes, the inward migration on a vast scale of non-Welsh speakers and the alarmingly swift erosion of traditional *mores*. Equally disconcerting has been the strange death of industrial Wales. The humming bustle of the Glamorganshire valleys, so reminiscent of even my own youth, is now a thing of the past. Since the 1970s and 80s the heavy industries of steel, tinplate and coal have been replaced by service industries of a much lighter nature. Above all the sense of community, so characteristic of earlier generations whether in the country or the towns, has been dissolved in the technological acids of a media-satiated world. Underlying all this has been a loss of an overall vision which previously, and for all its weakness, religion had provided. Modernity has yielded to an atomized, individualistic post-modernism in which transcendence has disappeared and the only values are transitory. Gwenallt did not live to see the economic and political dislocation of the 1970s, the brash Thatcherite capitalism of the 80s and the intractable problems following the collapse of the Eastern Bloc in the 90s which have all but decimated the values of Christian Europe whose civilization he prized so highly.

Yet for all this enough remains of Gwenallt's vision to make it relevant to the challenges of a new millennium. Just as his potent synthesis of tradition and innovation, Christianity and Marxism, rurality and urban life, the nation and the human community as a whole provided us with a beacon during the twentieth century, following the centenary of his birth it can do so still. 'He is our national poet of the century', stated Ned Thomas a generation ago, 'not because he celebrates Wales but he expresses the passions and tensions at work here without leaving anything out.'[9] It was a wholeness achieved through much mental turmoil and spiritual travail but in the end affirmative, jubilant and triumphant. What is more, for those who have the courage to believe, it is available still.

> *O'i waed Ef y daw tangnefedd,*
> *O'i Groes i bob oes yr hedd.*

> From His blood flows our peace
> From his Cross, to all ages, tranquility.

'T. Gwynn Jones', Eples

PART TWO

Selected Poems of Gwenallt

translated and annotated by
Patrick Thomas

1. Cwm yr Eglwys

In Cwm yr Eglwys only one wall remains
  Of the church by the sea's ancient pride.
Another Seithennin unloosed the waves
  That flow over her altar and chancel.

Will You, blessed Saviour,
  Sweep back the ocean?
The waters that mocked the foolish king
  Won't laugh at You.

And then we shall rebuild Your temple,
  Altar and chancel and choir:
And we'll turn the shameful marsh of the Cwm
  To a fruitful garden, where the sea once was.

(*Eples*, 1951)

Notes

Cwm yr Eglwys ('The Valley of the Church') is near Dinas in north Pembrokeshire. It takes its name from the church of St Brynach, which was washed into the sea during a terrible storm in 1859. Only the west wall of the building survived.

Seithennin A central character in the legend of *Cantre'r Gwaelod* (also known as *Maes Gwyddno*), the lost land in Cardigan Bay. He was in charge of the floodgates on which the kingdom's survival depended. His drunken neglect of them on a night when a high tide coincided with a horrendous storm led to the drowning of *Cantre'r Gwaelod*. The earliest reference to him comes in a series of Welsh stanzas in a thirteenth-century manuscript.

foolish king Seithennin is sometimes described as a king, though more often as a vassal of King Gwyddno. Gwenallt may also be hinting at the story of Canute and the waves. The Welsh idiom for 'to mock' or 'to laugh at' is *chwerthin am ben rhywun* (literally 'to laugh at someone's head'). Gwenallt says that the waters won't laugh at Christ's head (*Dy Ben Di* – 'Thy Head' – which to a Welsh speaker recalls the familiar phrase *Pen Calfaria* – 'The Head of Calvary' – with its crown of thorns) whereas they will laugh at the king's head (with its golden crown). This echoes Paul's remark about the foolishness of God being wiser than men (1 Cor. 1:25).

2. The Lady's Communion

She is the Spring, blessed Mary,
   Her energy, humour and order;
She chucked the winter and all its darkness
   Behind her virginal back.

The song of the coulter and the flow of the harrow
   Came to fields between Gwynedd and Gwent,
And like my grandfather in Llanfihangel Rhos y Corn
   I'll go to her Communion, her supper for rent.

There'll be *cawl* there and meat and vegetables,
   And several sorts of pudding on the table,
And the Lady herself coming round with a glass
   Of wine for each tenant before going away.

(Eples, 1951)

Notes

coulter 'The iron blade fixed in front of the share in a plough' (*SOED*) – *cwlltwr* in Welsh.

Gwynedd and Gwent The most north-westerly and south-easterly areas of Wales, signifying the land as a whole.

Llanfihangel Rhos y Corn ('The Church of Michael on the Moor of the Cairns') is a medieval church on the mountain between Brechfa and Llanybydder in north Carmarthenshire in the area where Gwenallt's grandparents lived.

supper for rent Every year the landlord of a rural Welsh estate would invite his tenants to a *cinio rhent* ('rent supper'), usually in a local pub which also belonged to him. The tenants would pay their rent and then be given a feast in return.

cawl (pronounced like the English 'cowl') A broth, usually made with a mutton bone, leeks and other vegetables. It is a basic part of the traditional South Wales diet, as well as being served on festive occasions (particularly *Gŵyl Ddewi* – St David's Day).

3. All Souls' Eve

On All Souls' Eve
The curtain between two worlds will be so thin
That a row of faces will come on it, one after the
    other,
Like a film of faces on the television set.

Amongst them two faces will be especially clear;
Two faces of two industrial women from the South;
Two faces which are now fine and full of grace
As in heaven they praise their Sustainer,
Who upheld them bravely in the fire of widowhood,
And in the dust and molten flow that broke their staff
    of life.

Before disappearing they clapped their hands with joy.

(*Gwreiddiau*, 1959)

Notes

dust and molten flow The first widow's husband died from a lung disease (probably pneumoconiosis) caused by the dust which he breathed while working in a coal mine. The second widow is Gwenallt's mother, Mari Jones. The 'molten flow' is a reference to the horrific industrial accident which killed her husband. In 1927, aged sixty, he received appalling burns from a spill of molten metal in the steel works where he was employed. He died in hospital a few hours later.

their staff of life The Welsh idiom used by Gwenallt is *ffon bara* (literally 'staff of bread'). The two dead men were the breadwinners for their households.

4. Wales

The dust of all the saints of the ages
    And the martyrs lies in your lap,
You gave them breath
    And you took it back.

The angels walked here,
    Their footprints are on your roads,
And the Holy Spirit nested,
    Like a dove, in your trees.

Poets heard in wind and breeze
    The cry of His sacrifice, His shout of pain,
And in the middle of your forests
    They saw the Wood of the Cross.

His resurrection was your spring,
    And your summer his verdant salvation,
And in the winter of your mountains
    He built tabernacles of grace.

The dew and rain of Providence filtered
    Onto your fields of corn and oats,
And his Glory was on the tackle
    And the bridles of your horses.

Your boats and your sailing ships
    Travelled the ocean's paths,
And their holds were laden with
    The merchandise of Calvary.

God made you to be his handmaid,
    He called you as a witness,
And printed His covenant
    On your entrances and doorposts.

Your saints are a splendid host,
   You love them, they love you,
And you will gather them under your wings
   As a hen gathers her chicks.

(*Ysgubau'r Awen*, 1939)

5. St David (Dewi Sant)

There is no border between two worlds in the
    Church;
The Church militant on earth is the same
As the victorious Church in Heaven.
And the saints will be in the two-one Church.
They will come to worship with us, a little
    congregation,
The saints, our oldest ancestors,
Who built Wales on the foundation of
The Cradle, the Cross and the Empty Grave;
And they will go out as before to wander through
    their old familiar places
And bring the Gospel to Wales.
I saw David strolling from county to county like
    God's gypsy
With the Gospel and the Altar in his caravan;
And coming to us to the Colleges and schools
To show the purpose of learning.
He went down to the bottom of the pit with the
    miners
And threw the light of his wise lamp on the coal-
    face;
On the platform of the steel works he put on the
    goggles and the little blue shirt
And showed the Christian being purified like the
    metal in the furnace;
And led the industrial proletariat to his unrespectable
    Church.
He carried his Church everywhere
As a body, which was life and brain and will
That did little and great things.
He brought the Church to our homes,
Put the Holy Vessels on the kitchen table,

And got bread from the pantry and bad wine from
  the cellar,
And stood behind the table like a tramp
Lest he should hide the wonder of the Sacrifice from
  us.
And after Communion we chatted by the fireside,
And he spoke to us about God's natural Order,
The person, the family, the nation and the society of
  nations,
And the Cross keeping us from turning one of them
  into a god.
He said that God shaped our nation
For His Own purpose,
And her death would impair that Order.
Anger furrowed his forehead
As he lashed us for licking the arse of the English
  Leviathan,
And letting ourselves, in his Christian country,
Be turned into Pavlov's dogs.
We asked him for his forgiveness, his strength and his
  ardour
And, before he left us, told him
To give the Lord Jesus Christ our poor
  congratulations,
And ask Him if we could come to Him
To praise Him forever in Heaven,
When that longed for moment comes
And we have to say 'Good night' to the world.

(*Eples*, 1951)

Notes

St David (Dewi Sant) The sixth-century ascetic who founded a community at what is now St David's in Pembrokeshire and has become
the patron saint of Wales. A large number of churches in the southern
half of Wales are dedicated to him, suggesting that he and his

followers formed a major evangelistic movement. His influence extended to Brittany, Cornwall and south-west England.

little and great things The Book of the Anchorite of Llanddewibrefi (a manuscript dating from 1346) contains *Buchedd Dewi*, a Welsh life of St David based on an earlier Latin work. Its version of David's final message has played an important part in shaping Welsh spirituality: 'Lords, brothers and sisters, be joyful and keep your faith and your belief, and do the little things that you have heard and seen from me.'

6. The Chapel in Carmarthenshire

The Sabbaths in Zion were so well-mannered,
The Chapel was so natural in the countryside;
The Chapel that was alive with the Gospel
And warm with the hymns of Pantycelyn, Dafydd
    Jones of Caeo,
Thomas Lewis of Tal-y-llychau and the County's
    hymnwriters.
Outside it were the farmers' vehicles
And in the stable built onto it horses would stamp
In the middle of prayers and sermons;
And around it the fields in August
Were laden with corn and oats and barley.
There was only a wall between the Saviour in the
    Chapel
And the Creator of the world outside.
The Chapel in the industrial South was so different,
Competing with the steel works, the tinplate works
    and the pit.

Yet, despite this, the Chapel gave without discrimination,
Both in the rural rain and greenness, and the noise
    and fog,
Water on a forehead, the ring on a finger and the
    resurrection above the coffin.

(*Gwreiddiau*, 1959)

Notes

Zion (*Seion* in the original Welsh spelling) A common name for a
Nonconformist chapel in Wales as in England.

Pantycelyn, Dafydd Jones of Caeo, Thomas Lewis of Tal-y-llychau
Three great Carmarthenshire hymnwriters from the Welsh Methodist

revival. William Williams of Pantycelyn (1717–91) was an Anglican deacon. He was deprived of his curacy because of his Methodist leanings and the Bishop of St David's refused to ordain him priest. He became a prolific and influential hymnwriter, whose work is still sung and appreciated ('Guide me, O thou great Redeemer' is a translation of one of his hymns). He was also the author of several major works of Welsh religious prose and poetry, and was a valued spiritual director. Dafydd Jones (1711–77) was a cattle drover from the village of Caeo (Caio). Several of his Welsh versions of hymns by Isaac Watts and his own original compositions remain popular. Thomas Lewis (1759–1842), the village blacksmith of Tal-y-llychau (Talley), is remembered for a powerful and moving hymn about the suffering of Christ.

7. The Door

Like the seven men once in Harlech and Gwales
   We were in the three-doored hall above the sea,
Listening to the song of the aesthetic birds,
   Beside which every other song was harsh.

The sun did not penetrate through its romantic
      windows
   On the ecstasy of the dandified Khayyamish feasts;
And the candleflame of flesh through the centuries
      danced in it:
   Helen and Salome and *La Belle Dame*.

But Heilyn opened the obstinate door:
   And we heard the shriek of the land in its pain,
The red barking of the industrial dust;
   And saw the bread, the wine and the Cross.

(*Gwreiddiau*, 1959)

Notes

the seven men once in Harlech and Gwales In *Branwen*, the second of the four 'branches' of the *Mabinogion* (the early Welsh collection of legends), only seven Welsh warriors survive from the expedition to Ireland to rescue their maltreated princess. The men spend seven years feasting at Harlech in North Wales. There they are entertained by three birds who sing them a song which makes every other song that they have ever heard seem unlovely in comparison with it (hence Gwenallt's reference to 'the song of the aesthetic birds beside which every other song was harsh'). The seven warriors then move on to Gwales (the island of Grassholm off the Pembrokeshire coast). There there is a hall with two open doors and a third which is closed. They have been told that they can stay on the island as long as they do not open this third door. They spend eighty delightful years on

Gwales, without remembering for a moment the horrors they have seen, or their own sufferings, or any sorrow that is in the world. In all that time none of them seems a day older.

Heilyn opened the obstinate door In the end his curiosity proves too much for Heilyn, one of the seven warriors. He opens the forbidden door to see if what has been said about it is really true. Immediately the seven men are overwhelmed by the memory of all the awful things that have happened to them and their former companions. Filled with sadness they leave the island of Gwales never to return.

8. The Old Hymns

They sang above my cradle,
Over my boyhood and my youth,
Like a choir of Christian birds:
They and their song carried Calvary
And the cross to the centre of the workplaces;
Bethlehem and the cradle to the centre of the
    coal-tips;
The empty grave among the wagons,
And brought the river Jordan without vitriol in its
    water.

I hunted these birds from the forest,
Aiming my scientific gun;
Chased them from the brushwood and the
    undergrowth
With my positive, materialist cudgel:
But I would hear their song from other forests
Like a choir of soft, dark, foul-dunged owls.

In the drought and wilderness of the forest
They continued to sing under the roots of the trees,
Under the threshold of reason and the doorstep of
    understanding,
Still singing although I didn't hear them;
But I know now that they persisted in singing
Perseveringly, assiduously, inexorably.

And when the light came back to the forest
They rose up from amongst the roots to the branches
    and the tree tops
To sing again, and their song had matured in the
    night:

Bringing the cradle, the Cross, the empty grave and
  Pentecost
Back again, fierily new;
And under the drops of blood and water
Kissing His victorious feet,
Without daring from guilt to look at the terrible
  holiness of His face.

(*Gwreiddiau*, 1959)

9. Judas Iscariot

The group of simpletons needed your skill
To keep accounts and gather money in,
John wasn't bothered, Peter didn't care
That gold was needed to bring God closer:
The frequent handouts milked the money chest,
And Easter's wine and food cleared it right out,
And in the marketplace you sold your Christ
Knowing that you'd escape from their snare and net.
It's a pity that you hanged before the Son of Man
    rose up
And shared the wine and unleavened bread a second
    time,
The Cross lifting your treachery from your lip
And washing your dirty money to a perfect shine;
You could, like Peter, have wept bitterly
And seen the coffer full at Pentecost.

(Ysgubau'r Awen, 1959)

10. Wales

Yes, we swore at you and lashed you;
Called you a pain, a bitch and a whore,
    Claimed that your body was cancerous and scabby:
Forgive us if we were too harsh to you,
For we are neither infallible prophets nor just saints:
    Our bodies and our souls are not healthy.

Through centuries you were like an oak tree sucking
        nourishment from the earth,
And light from above; but today you've forgotten the
        sky
    And live to claw small idols from the earth:
Your religion is the slack sympathy of the historical
        Jesus;
Your Christmas is toys and cards; your Easter is
        chocolate eggs:
    The lily without the thorns and thistles; the light
        without the fire.

We must throw ourselves and you into the
        sackclothed lake;
A lake whose waters are serious; whose banks are
        white as salt;
    With the wind on its surface like a despairing cry:
And then we shall walk together to the holy Supper,
And ask on our knees before taking the wine and
        bread:
    'Jesus, son of David, have mercy on us.'

And afterwards, like Isaac, we shall pull out the earth
        from the wells,
The earth that was put there to choke them by the
        Philistines, the gold-milked farmers,

The jacks-in-office, the sycophants and the traitors
        of every kind:
And we shall dig in the valleys for the flowing springs;
The well of Moses and the Maccabees, of Glyndŵr
        and Ambrosius
And the wells that have their source in God's grace
        and salvation.

(*Gwreiddiau*, 1959)

Note

Glyndŵr and Ambrosius Owain Glyndŵr (*c.* 1354–*c.* 1416) led a rebellion against English rule in 1400. His followers proclaimed him Prince of Wales and by 1405 the whole of the country was under his control. In the next few years he suffered a series of reverses. By 1413 the revolt had collapsed and he was in hiding. The *daroganwyr* (prophetic poets) continued to claim that Owain would return to rescue Wales and he has become the archetypal Welsh national hero. Emrys Wledig or Ambrosius (mid- to late fifth century) was the leader of the British/Welsh army that defeated the Anglo-Saxon invaders at the battle of Mynydd Baddon (Badon Hill or *Mons Badonicus*). He is the only British/Welsh general to be mentioned by the sixth-century Welsh historian Gildas. His victory halted the Anglo-Saxon advance for several decades.

11. Bishop William Morgan

He saw that Welsh was only the common dialect
 Of fair and farm, ballad and harp and tune;
And that the tongue that chattered in Monmouth's
  markets couldn't understand
 The guttural tongue of the markets of Anglesey.

Before him he found his people in the Church's
  pews
 Sitting beyond the boundaries of grace,
Like the sheep and lambs of his home left to wander
  starving
 On alien mountains without a blade of grass.

And so he strove to release the Sacred Library
 From ancient Hebrew skin and Greek papyri:
The Welsh heard the Father, the Son and the Spirit
 Speak in Welsh for the first time – an astounding
  grace.

Salvation from Monmouth to Anglesey came from
  eavesdropping
 On the Messiah's words and actions in ordinary,
  beautiful prose:
And hearing him blessing the wine and bread in the
  Upper Room,
 Dying, rising, ascending in the poet's noble
  language.

We praise him for his perseverance, his bravery and
  his sanctity
 And for his help in keeping the nation and the
  literary language alive,

Giving it dignity and the highest honour
  By turning it into one of the dialects of God's
  Revelation.

(*Gwreiddiau*, 1959)

Notes

Bishop William Morgan (1545–1604) was a gifted Greek, Hebrew and Latin scholar, as well as being fluent in Welsh and English. He was responsible for the first complete translation of the Bible into Welsh in 1588. At the time he was vicar of Llanrhaeadr-ym-Mochnant in Denbighshire. He later became bishop of Llandaff and then of St Asaph. In the late sixteenth century all but a small minority of the people of Wales spoke no other language but Welsh and Morgan's translation had a quite remarkable impact. It received an ecstatic welcome from the Welsh poets and writers of his time. Morgan had created a standard Welsh, comprehensible throughout Wales, that became the literary language used by later authors. As well as transforming the spiritual and cultural life of Wales, William Morgan's Bible has been credited with saving and preserving the Welsh language and Welsh national identity in the centuries that followed its publication. In 1599 he produced a revision of *Llyfr Gweddi Gyffredin* (the Welsh Book of Common Prayer) on which all later versions were based.

Monmouth . . . Anglesey Two Welsh counties – one in the far south-east and the other in the far north-west – whose colloquial Welsh dialects differed greatly in William Morgan's time.

12. Rhydcymerau

The saplings of the third world war were planted
On the land of Esgeir-ceir and the fields of Tir-bach
Near Rhydcymerau.

I remember my grandmother in Esgeir-ceir
Sitting by the fire and pleating her apron;
The skin of her face as dry and yellow as the Peniarth
    manuscript,
And the Welsh on her aged lips the Welsh of
    Pantycelyn.
She was a part of the Puritanical Wales of the last
    century.
My grandfather, although I never saw him,
Was a 'character'; a little creature, lively, tough,
    limping,
And fond of his pint;
He was an eighteenth century vagabond.
They raised nine children,
Poets, elders and Sunday School teachers,
Leaders in the small circles that they moved in.

Uncle Dafydd used to farm Tir-bach,
A country poet and a local rhymester,
His song to the little cockerel was famous
    thereabouts:
'The little cockerel scratching
    This end, that end of the garden.'
We used to go to him on our summer holidays
To tend the sheep and fashion lines of alliterative
    poetry,
Englynion and eight line verses to the eight-seven
    measure.
He raised eight children.

The eldest son was a minister with the Calvinistic
  Methodists,
And he too wrote poetry.
Our family was a nestful of poets.

And now there are only trees there,
With their impudent roots sucking the old earth:
Trees where there was a community,
Forest where there were farms,
The ragged slang of the Southern English where there
  was poetry and theology,
The bark of foxes where children and lambs once
  cried.
And in the darkness at its centre
Is the den of the English Minotaur;
And on trees, as on crosses,
The skeletons of poets, chapel elders, ministers and
  Sunday School teachers
Bleaching in the sun,
And being washed by the rain and dried by the wind.

(Eples, 1951)

Notes

Rhydcymerau is a village between Llanybydder and Llansawel in
Carmarthenshire. After the First World War a group of local land-
lords sold a large part of their estates to the Forestry Commission
and the Brechfa Forest was created. In the decades that followed the
Forestry Commission planted the farms with conifers (trees that were
not native to the area), the tenant farmers had to move elsewhere
and in many cases the houses that had been their homes were dyna-
mited, so that it was as if they had never existed. Gwenallt had
spent his childhood Easter and summer holidays with his relatives
at Esgeir-ceir and Tir-bach, the two farms which he mentions. His
poem is an angry lament at the destruction of a community which,
although economically marginal, had a quite remarkable spiritual
and cultural wealth.

the Peniarth manuscript The seventeenth-century antiquary Robert Vaughan of Hengwrt built up a unique collection of early Welsh manuscripts of poetry and prose. By the nineteenth century this belonged to the Wynne family of Peniarth. The collection, now in the National Library of Wales, thus became known as the 'Peniarth manuscripts'. Gwenallt's comparison links his grandmother with the very beginnings of Welsh culture.

the Welsh of Pantycelyn William Williams of Pantycelyn (1717–91), the most important Welsh hymnwriter, often used Carmarthenshire Welsh dialect words and idioms in his works. Gwenallt's grandmother spoke the same dialect as Pantycelyn and had inherited the spiritual tradition which he had helped to found.

the Puritanical Wales of the last century Victorian Welsh Nonconformity put a strong emphasis on Sabbatarianism and teetotalism.

elders and Sunday School teachers 'Elders' is a translation of *blaenoriaid*. These are the elected and ordained elders of Calvinistic Methodist chapels. The Calvinistic Methodists (known officially as the Presbyterian Church of Wales) trace their origin to the eighteenth-century spiritual revival led by Daniel Rowland, Howel Harris and William Williams. They ordained their own ministers for the first time in 1811, breaking away from what was then the Church of England in Wales. Welsh Sunday Schools were attended (and still are in some places) by adults as well as children. The adult classes would discuss theological matters, with the help of *esboniadau* (Bible commentaries), which were best-selling books in nineteenth- and early twentieth-century Wales. During a period when little or no Welsh was taught in day schools (and when they discouraged the language to such an extent that pupils were often punished for speaking it) the Sunday Schools had an additional importance. They enabled the people of Rhydcymerau and similar communities to become literate and highly articulate in their mother-tongue, the language of their homes, their worship and their everyday lives. A Sunday School teacher was thus a very valuable and highly valued individual in the culture which Gwenallt describes.

a country poet and a local rhymester Gwenallt's uncle, Dafydd Ehedydd Jones, had a considerable reputation as a *bardd gwlad* – a 'country poet' who would compose verses in Welsh on the occasion of births, marriages, deaths in the local community. His most famous ballad (about a mysterious death in the woods near Llanfihangel

Rhos y Corn) is still treasured by some of the Welsh-speaking families who remain in the area. The 'song to the little cockerel' was recorded by the Rhydcymerau singer Angharad Davies in 1989.

lines of alliterative poetry The original has *llinellau cynghanedd*. *Cynghanedd* is the system of alliteration and internal rhyme which governs traditional Welsh poetry. *Englynion* are short poems written in a strict pattern of *cynghanedd*.

13. Catholicity

He was imprisoned by His flesh and His Jewish bones
    Within the borders of His homeland,
  But he gave them like living planks to be
       hammered,
  And they were raised from the grave by His Father,
    In spite of the watchers, as a catholic body.

And since then Cardiff is as close as Calvary,
    And Bangor every inch as Bethlehem,
  The storms are stilled on Cardigan Bay,
  And on every street the lunatics
    Can find salvation from the fringe of His hem.

He didn't hide His Gospel in the clouds of Judea,
    Beyond the tongue and eyes of man.
  But he gives the life that lasts forever
  In a sip of wine and a morsel of bread,
    And the gift of the Spirit in drops of water.

(*Y Coed*, 1969)

14. Choosing

When I used to live in the world of romanticism and
idealism
I lived in the middle of a woolly mist in the sky above
the world:
If there was a God, he would come through the mist
like a neon light,
And I wasn't sure that I was myself;
I'd grasp my nose to see if it was a nose
And not wool; and my toes
To see if they were part of my feet and not toes of
mist;
I supposed that I was only a wisp of mist
Or a scrap of wool, and when I tried to grasp the
mist
It disappeared between my fingers like an illusion.
My life was so comfortable and pointless
That I could easily have killed myself.
The view above the world was so splendid,
Watching mist moving and growing through the
centuries,
Growing by fighting against another mist,
And the greatest battle was to crucify the mist on
Calvary.
I got tired of the mist because it was insubstantial
food
And wool couldn't plumb the inner depths.

It was a revolution to set foot on the solid earth;
To shake hands with a man; to kiss a girl;
To sit with the family by the fire;
To drink witty wine with friends,
And the stink of a pigsty was a delight.
To discover that I was living in the twentieth century,

Living in a particular parish
And in a particular country named Wales.
I had to see that I was myself
By choosing with the intellect, the passions and the
    will
Between night and day, between God and devil,
Between necessity and freedom and between sin and
    grace.
And having chosen, to shape the life of a parish,
To help the history of Wales and worship in a
    Church.
And when I looked up into the sky
Where once was abstract mist and insubstantial wool,
I saw a solid Star standing still above a Baby's cradle.

(*Gwreiddiau*, 1959)

15. The Lord's Supper

There was infection in the air and things looked
  bad,
All nature's colours were edged with an inky stain,
And a shepherd on the hillside was gathering his
  sheep and counting them,
Counting the stupid sheep of maggoty, putrid sins.

It was quiet in the Church, and there was terror in
  the silence,
Terror from the altar and the Cross and the east in
  the glass,
And the chancel so strangely distant and the ceiling so
  high above,
And we in the hollow kneeling like dark and dirty
  clods.

Bethlehem came down from heaven to the middle of
  the Communion service,
With its angels and shepherds and dumb, unwilling
  animals,
And Mary tidily tying God's immortality in his nappy,
And rocking eternity to sleep in his cradle.

He didn't chuck our bit of flesh like a rag on the
  rubbish tips of Gehenna,
Or throw our blood there like a bottle of dried up
  medicine,
But raised them from the grip of the worms'
  matchless three days
As a transparent spiritual body, the perfection of God
  and man.

The sound of falling water in the chancel was like a
    city square in Italy,
Flowing along the bed of ritual and devotion from
    heaven's fountains
And a ray of light playing around the cross, dimming
    the two candles,
A ray from the pyre of His divine humanity.

And outside the deadly darkness of the yew tree in
    Llanbadarn turned
To a spring of green overflowing with song,
And the sea raced to embrace the Rheidol and the
    Ystwyth,
With its foam aflame and its waves all on fire.

                                        (*Y Coed*, 1969)

Notes

the Church During his time as an Anglican Gwenallt worshipped in
the large and beautiful medieval church of Llanbadarn Fawr, outside
Aberystwyth.

and the east in the glass This is what is in *Y Coed* ('*a'r dwyrain yn
y gwydr*'). The volume was published posthumously and many of
the poems may not be in their final form. One is tempted to change
the words round to '*a'r gwydr yn y dwyrain*' ('and the glass in the
east'), which would apparently make better sense – and yet may not
be what the poet intended.

the Rheidol and the Ystwyth The two rivers that flow into the sea
at Aberystwyth.

16. Germany's Children

In Germany Rachel still
   Weakly, silently weeps:
Herod's sword was more merciful
   Than the famine on the Rhine, on the Ruhr.

These arms of bone are nursing
   A bundle of dry bones,
There's not much food in her pantry
   Nor a drop of milk in her breast.

And the men are busy digging
   The vengeful earth and clay,
The biers will be lighter
   Because the coffins are a good bit smaller.

The crucified Christ's pity
   Streams from His side and his feet;
Every funeral is a thorn in His skull,
   Every grave a drop of blood.

(*Eples*, 1951)

Note

In Germany The poem refers to conditions in Germany immediately
after the end of the Second World War.

17. Good Friday

I went for a walk on Good Friday afternoon
  Through the fields of a farm to see the lambs,
To see the first lambs of the season,
  Skin wrapped scraps of innocence and mischief.
And there were twelve sheep and lambs there
  And a ram, who had set themselves out, each one,
As if an artist had been there arranging them
  Before painting their picture.

Suddenly the bearded Shepherd came among them,
  And I didn't know where He came from;
From a painting by an artist in Ravenna,
From an Oratorio by Bach,
From a chapter in John's Gospel,
  Or from heaven.

Gradually His shepherd's crook became a Cross,
And I heard the thorns shouting in His head,
  And the nails crying out in His hands and feet:
And then I saw the twelve, lambs and sheep
And an unnecessary, unentangled ram,
  Red with the blood.

(*Gwreiddiau*, 1959)

18. Easter Sunday

Holy Week is the world's sacred Winter:
  The earth is a widow, the skies are sere,
There's a sound of scourging and nailing in the
    vinegary wind;
  And the darkness chokes the Son of Man.

But spring, two springs, are coming to the world
  From the depths on the third morning:
The lily, the primrose and the daffodil
  Will follow the Saviour from the Egypt of soil.

The rejoicing is green and white, the praise is yellow
  Because the new Adam has risen alive from the
    grave;
And the ivy, tying itself round the tree like the old
    serpent,
  Is for us eternal life with God.

(Gwreiddiau, 1959)

19. The Homes of the Workers

The camps that were built by Mammon's architect
In the valley and on the hillsides
   Were incomparable homes;
In the gaseous, metallic sea,
With its ebb and flow of flames,
   They were the islands of blessedness.

Talking was so easy after the machine,
Food was so sweet after the slaving,
   And every drink was better than wine:
His children and his wife were miracles;
The hearth was Christianity and culture;
   The human family was civilization.

That home in Nazareth
Was like our homes,
   A worker's home, according to the Word:
Give thanks that the Messiah was a worker,
That a craftsman died on the Cross
   And that Mary was a worker's mother.

(Gwreiddiau, 1959)

20. Time

The clock on the mantelpiece is cruelly round,
    The roundness of sun and moon and all the science
      of heaven;
And our petty little life, for all our noise and fuss and
      boasting,
    Is only the fingers' silent movement on its
    roundness.

We came from the womb beneath its small
      pendulum's dictatorship,
    When the hour comes we'll fall to the grave on its
      fingers' sign:
And between these fingers Nature also sows and reaps
      and dies:
    Civilizations rise, and kingdoms fall.

In the Evangelical Calendar that hangs beneath it on
      the wall
    Time moves like a line from step to step;
And through His journey from heaven to the womb,
      and from the Cross to His father's breast
    We are lifted from the circle, above the fingers'
    dictatorship.

                                (*Gwreiddiau*, 1959)

21. The Church of the Pater Noster

On the Mount of Olives is the Church of the Pater
  Noster;
A Church on the spot where, according to tradition,
Our Lord taught His Prayer to his disciples,
His own pattern of Prayer.
The Lord's Prayer is there in forty four languages;
And the first language is Syriac,
A language which is not much different, so they say,
From Aramaic, the language our Saviour spoke.
Amongst them was the prayer in Welsh,
The Welsh Pater Noster;
Welsh in the Church on the Mount of Olives;
The greatest privilege it has had.
Thank God for Welsh,
One of Europe's most Christian languages,
One of the dialects of the Trinity.
Its vocabulary is Christmas;
Its syntax is Calvary;
Its grammar is the grammar of the Empty Grave;
And its phonetics are Hosannas.

(*Y Coed*, 1969)

22. Importance

Yes, their pictures in the brittle papers show
   That there are very important people in Wales:
Parliamentarians asking expensive questions
   And boasting when an Election draws near.
Patriots at a St David's Day Dinner
   Mixing soap with water and food:
People receiving the Queen's honours
   Standing like well-dressed idols by the Gate.
Poets shaping classics
   And competing in the literary race:
Half gods who go berserk
   At any unpleasant criticism.
Here, by Pilate's court,
   They can be put in their place;
Measured with a yardstick, weighed in the scales;
   The eternal yardstick and scales of heaven.
The most important by far are the insignificant priest
   Praising Mary in a town somewhere:
And the never-mentioned Minister in the depths of the
     country
   In his poverty preaching the Word.

(*Y Coed*, 1969)

Notes

a St David's Day Dinner A *Cinio Gŵyl Ddewi* or St David's Day
Dinner is often an occasion for ostentatious expressions of Welsh
patriotism by establishment figures.

soap The Welsh word for 'to flatter' is *seboni* (literally 'to soap').

23. Glamorganshire and Carmarthenshire

Thomas Lewis of Tal-y-llychau,
    With the sound of his hammer in the forge like bells
Ringing over the village and the monastery and the
        swans on the lake;
    He pulled his hymn like a horseshoe from the fire,
    And struck it on the anvil of the Holy Spirit
Putting in it the nails of Calvary's Hill.

    Williams of Pantycelyn would come
    By my elbow in Llansadwrn,
To teach me to sing in his song's furrows;
    But I lost the bleating about His visage
    On top of a soapbox on the town square
And His sweet voice was shattered by the ball of the crane.

    The industrial proletariat couldn't
    Wander through the works like a pilgrim,
With its pocket empty and the burden on its back:
    On Saturday nights we cried out for justice
    And sang your hymns on Sunday nights:
Mabon and Caeo; Keir Hardie and Crug-y-bar.

    The span of the Cross is much greater
    Than their Puritanism and their Socialism
And there's a place for the fist of Karl Marx in His
        Church:
    The farm and the furnace will exist together on
        His estate,
    The humanism of the coal-mine, the godliness of
        the countryside:
Tawe and Tywi, Canaan and Wales, earth and heaven.

(Eples, 1951)

Notes

Thomas Lewis (1759–1842) The village blacksmith in the Carmarthenshire village of Tal-y-llychau (Talley). He wrote a famous Welsh hymn about the suffering of Christ: '*Wrth gofio'i riddfannau'n yr ardd*' ('Remembering his groans in the garden').

the monastery and the swans on the lake The Lord Rhys, lord of Deheubarth, founded a Premonstratensian abbey at Talley in the late twelfth century. Its ruins are not far from the lake which gives the village its Welsh name Tal-y-llychau ('the end of the lakes').

Williams of Pantycelyn William Williams of Pantycelyn (1717–91), the great Carmarthenshire hymnwriter.

Llansadwrn A small village in rural Carmarthenshire.

His visage . . . His sweet voice . . . The references are to Christ as portrayed in Pantycelyn's hymns.

like a pilgrim The idea of the Christian as a pilgrim plays a major part in Pantycelyn's work.

the burden on its back Gwenallt is recalling the opening lines of one of Pantycelyn's best known hymns: '*Mi dafla' 'maich oddi ar fy ngwar wrth deimlo dwyfol loes . . .*' ('I throw my burden from my back, feeling divine pain . . .').

Mabon The nickname of William Abraham (1842–1922), one of greatest leaders of the South Wales miners and their first Member of Parliament. He was MP for the Rhondda from 1885 to 1918 and for Rhondda West from 1918 to 1922. In 1898 he became the first president of the South Wales Miners' Federation.

Caeo is a reference to Dafydd Jones (1711–77), the hymnwriter from the Carmarthenshire village of Caeo (Caio).

Keir Hardie James Keir Hardie (1856–1915), the first leader of the Labour Party, was Member of Parliament for the Glamorgan constituency of Merthyr from 1900 until his death.

Crug-y-bar A small Carmarthenshire village which gave its name to a famous hymn tune that is often sung at Welsh funerals.

Tawe and Tywi Two rivers: the Tawe flows through the industrial areas of the Swansea valley in Glamorganshire and the Tywi (Towy) flows through rural Carmarthenshire.

24. The Church

The Church is tents pitched on the side of the Mount
    of Transfiguration,
  Tents where Peter wanted his tents to be,
On the Mountain where Christ shone like the sun on
    the snow,
  Without the snow cooling the sun and without the
  sun melting the snow.

We were once in the valley thundering from our
    soapboxes
  Against the workers' Egypt and the bosses'
  strawless bricks,
Asking Engels and Karl Marx, instead of Christ on
    the Mountain,
  To lead us to the Communist Canaan at the
  journey's end.

We saw the pattern of the universe through a
    laboratory window in the valley,
  A pattern like a carpet's with a pile of shattered
  atoms;
Efnisien was Elijah and Matholwch was Moses,
  Jesus was the ventriloquist who spoke from God's
  cloud.

We climbed to the Mountain with Hegel, and a Spirit
    Christ was there,
  A cradleless, graveless, colourless, shapeless
  fragment of the Absolute,
Turning hills and valleys to mountains and the
    mountains going up like steps
  From the lowest in prehistory to the Himalayas of
  human perfection.

Canaan is a new Egypt, the atomic bomb came from
    the carpet,
  And the woolly Absolute wouldn't walk through sin
    and the depths of being,
The canvas of the tents is too thick to see the sun in
    the snow,
  The snow will make the sun lukewarm, or the sun
    will yellow the snow.

When the Spirit thins the canvas we shall see that the
    universe is a creation,
  That the worker is a person because he is the child
    of God,
And see Christ rising up from his Cross and Grave
    like the glory
  Of the sun in the wounded snow to give light to the
    seventh Heaven.

(*Eples*, 1951)

Notes

Efnisien A brutally destructive character in the *Mabinogion* story of
Branwen. He stirs up mischief between the Irish and the Welsh by
mutilating the Irishmen's stallions. When the countries go to war
Efnisien outwits a group of Irish soldiers who are hiding in flour
bags, crushing their skulls with his fingers. In a later incident he
throws Branwen's little son into the fire. As a final act of repentance
for his appalling actions Efnisien jumps into the Cauldron of Rebirth
which the Irish have been using to resuscitate their troops. He breaks
it into pieces but kills himself in the process.

Matholwch The Irish king who marries Branwen, sister of Bendigeid-
fran, the giant ruler of Wales, in the *Mabinogion*. Matholwch's
mistreatment of Branwen eventually leads to a war between the
Welsh and the Irish which is disastrous for both sides.

25. Pigeons

The workers would tend their pigeons in the evening,
   After the day's drudgery, on the Bryn,
Every coop with its stage at the top of the garden
   Would release its white cloud.

They'd be sent to North Wales and England
   And released from their baskets to the heavens,
But they'd return from that far-off loveliness
   To our neighbourly poverty in the South.

In the sky they'd surround the pillars of smoke
   Giving colour to the crooked greyness;
Masses of beauty amidst the mist;
   The Holy Spirit's picture above the Valley.

The Holy Spirit sanctifying the smoke,
   And turning the worker into a living person,
Grace transforming capitalism
   And the Unions a part of God's family.

(Eples, 1951)

26. The Dead

Having turned fifty a man sees fairly clearly
  The people and surroundings that moulded his life,
And the steel ropes that bind me most tightly to them
  Are the graves in two cemeteries in one of the
    villages of the South.

Riding on bicycles stolen from scrap
  And playing Rugby for Wales with pigs' bladders,
I never dreamed that I'd hear of two of my friends
  Coughing up their lungs dirty red into a bucket.

Our neighbours were a family from Merthyr Tydfil,
  Our nickname for them was 'The Martyrs',
A cough shot five of them in their turn over the
    garden hedge
  To interrupt our talking and dampen our fun.

We'd sneak into the biblical parlours to peep in shock
  At charcoaled flesh in the coffin, and a voice of ashes,
We learnt there the collects of red rebellion and the
    litanies of violence
  Above coffin lids screwed down before their time.

Not the death that walks naturally like a gaoler
  With a warning in the clanking sound of his damp keys,
But the industrial leopard that leaps on working men,
  Suddenly and slyly from the midst of water and fire.

The hootered death: the dusty, choking, drunk death,
  The death with the terror of blue fate;
An explosion and a pit-flood would turn us to savages
    for a time,
  Fighting with catastrophic, primitive, hateful powers.

Brave, silent women with a fistful of blood money,
   And a bucketful of death as a lifelong memory,
Carrying coal, cutting firewood and doing the garden,
   Reading more often the story of the suffering on the
      Cross.

On Palm Sunday we'd put on their graves a posy
   Of silicotic roses and lilies as white as gas,
And gather between the untimely stones and the
      immature curb
The old curses and blasphemies from their funerals.

Utopia vanished from the top of Gellionnen,
   Abstract humanity, a classless, borderless world;
Today what remains at the back of the memory
   Is family and neighbourhood, the sacrifice and
      suffering of man.

                                             (*Eples*, 1951)

Notes

one of the villages of the South The village is Alltwen, across the
river Tawe from Pontardawe in the Swansea valley. It was a heavily
industrialized area. Gwenallt grew up there and took his bardic name
from it, reversing Alltwen into 'Gwenallt'.

'The Martyrs' The Welsh word for 'martyr' is *merthyr*. Merthyr
Tydfil gets its name from an early Welsh woman saint called Tydfil
who was martyred there.

the biblical parlours Traditional Welsh practice in both industrial
and rural areas was (and often still is) to put the coffin in the parlour
(the front room which was kept spotless and not normally used)
before a funeral. The first part of the funeral service would take
place in the house, usually using the big black family Bible.

silicotic roses and lilies as white as gas Many miners died from the
lung disease silicosis. Others were killed by gas explosions in the
mines.

27. Owain Glyndŵr

Owain retired to oblivion,
  As the chronicle bears witness,
It's a pity it didn't add
  Where and how this was:
Did he finally find shelter
  With Alis at Monnington Straddel?
Does he lie in the Chapel nearby
  In the English peace of the grave?
      But he rose after four centuries
      To begin his battle again.

His unlocked, unlatched mansion
  Was burnt to white ashes;
The doves were paralysed in the stone tower
  And the fish shivered in the lake:
The best woman of all women was taken
  To London, and two of his children,
And he was hunted like Grivas
  From hill to valley by oppressors:
      But he rose after four centuries
      To begin his battle again.

He demanded a Church for the Welsh
  Free from Canterbury's grip;
Two Colleges to be built for the scholars
  And Welsh-speaking Bishops for the saints:
And he reigned for a time as a king,
  In the way of the princes before him;
But the four lions were defeated
  And the stars, the rain and the wind;
      But he rose after four centuries
      To begin his battle again.

His Parliament is now an institute
  Where the town meetings are held,
And tables for playing billiards
  And a café have been put into it:
And there was recent talk of a row
  Between the narrow and the broadminded Welsh,
As to whether the café should open
  On a Sunday afternoon.
          But he will rise after centuries
          To open his Parliament again.

(*Gwreiddiau*, 1959)

Notes

Owain retired to oblivion In 1400 Owain Glyndŵr (*c.* 1354–*c.* 1416) led the great rebellion against English rule in Wales. A note in Peniarth MS 135 says that Owain went into hiding on St Matthew's Day in 1415 and that no one knows where he hid himself.

Alis at Monnington Straddel Alice Scudamore, Owain's daughter, lived at Monnington Straddel in Herefordshire. It has been suggested that he may have taken refuge with her and that his body may have been buried there.

unlocked, unlatched mansion Sycharth, Owain's home in the parish of Llansilin not far from the Shropshire border, was described in idyllic terms by Iolo Goch, one of the leading fourteenth-century Welsh poets. The reference to it as 'unlocked' and 'unlatched' comes from Iolo's poem, as do the doves, the fish and 'the best woman of all women' (Margaret Hanmer, Owain's wife). Sycharth was burned to the ground by the English in 1403.

hunted like Grivas Owain on the run is compared to the Greek Cypriot leader Giorgios Grivas (1898–1974) whose EOKA fighters waged a guerrilla war against the British in Cyprus in the 1950s.

a Church for the Welsh In a letter addressed to the king of France in 1406 Owain announced that he was transferring the allegiance of his restored principality of Wales from the Roman pope (supported by the English) to the Avignon pope (supported by the

French). His aim was to create a Welsh Church independent of Canterbury under an archbishop based at St David's.

Two Colleges Owain Glyndŵr also proposed establishing two universities in Wales, one in the north and one in the south.

Welsh-speaking Bishops for the saints In 1944 Gwenallt became an Anglican, being confirmed by Archbishop Prosser in his palace at Abergwili outside Carmarthen. In 1957 Alfred Morris, an Englishman who spoke no Welsh, was elected Archbishop of Wales. Gwenallt was so disgusted by this that he left the Church in Wales and returned to the Calvinistic Methodism in which he had been brought up. By stressing Owain's ideal he underlines his disapproval of the new archbishop.

he reigned for a time as a king Owain proclaimed himself Prince of Wales in 1400. He had taken possession of the whole country by 1405, but four years later only a limited area of north and mid-Wales remained under his control.

the four lions Owain adopted as his coat of arms the four lions of the house of Gwynedd, the former Princes of Wales.

his Parliament A reference to the building in Machynlleth, Powys, in which Owain Glyndŵr is believed to have convened a Welsh parliament in 1404.

28. Cwm Tryweryn

The moneyed Goliath rose up in Liverpool
  To shame and despoil the country people,
Gathering rivers together to drown
  The community at Tryweryn:
Come, David, with your river stones,
  And God behind your sling,
      To save the hymns of Capel Celyn,
      And the ballads of Bob Tai'r Felin
From being murdered by the water in the devil's dam.

Dewi, ask God in your prayers
  To save your people from the Philistines;
The two Llywelyns and Glyndŵr lead
  Your armies to Cwm Tryweryn:
And you, great Michael of Bodiwan,
  If you were in Bala now,
      The empty graveyard of Capel Celyn,
      Homes and crops and songs and harps would
        not
Be buried under the uncircumcised giant's dam.

(*Gwreiddiau*, 1959)

Notes

Cwm Tryweryn The Tryweryn valley is to the north of Bala in the old Merionethshire. In 1955 Liverpool Corporation announced that they were bringing a bill before Parliament to give the right to construct a dam and a reservoir. Under the plan the village of Capel Celyn with its houses, chapel, school and post office would be drowned, as would twelve other houses and farms. Of the 67 people in the district 48 would lose their homes. The final HMI inspection of Ysgol Celyn (Celyn School) in 1958 described Cwm Tryweryn as 'a thoroughly Welsh speaking area with proud traditions of musical and literary culture'. In November 1956 the people of Tryweryn marched through the streets of Liverpool carrying a huge banner with the slogan 'Your homes are safe, save ours – do not drown our homes'. Some of the onlookers hurled abuse and spat at them. All but one of the Welsh MPs opposed the bill in Parliament. Even so it was passed. Cwm Tryweryn disappeared beneath the reservoir. Anger at the fate of this small community was a major factor in the growth of Welsh nationalism and the electoral successes of Plaid Cymru in the 1960s and 70s.

the ballads of Bob Tai'r Felin Robert Roberts (1870–1951), better known as 'Bob Tai'r Felin', was a very popular folk singer who farmed at Cwm Tirmynach near Bala.

Dewi Dewi Sant (St David), the patron saint of Wales.

The Two Llywelyns and Glyndŵr Llywelyn the Great (1173–1240), prince of Gwynedd, Llywelyn ap Gruffydd (died 1282), prince of Wales, and Owain Glyndŵr, leader of the 1400 rebellion.

Michael of Bodiwan Michael D. Jones (1822–98) was the fiery principal of a theological college at Bodiwan, Bala, training ministers for the *Annibynwyr* (Welsh Independents or Congregationalists). His political views were both radical and Welsh nationalist and he played a leading part in the movement to establish a colony of Welsh speakers in Patagonia.

29. The Stumbling Block

We set the stone against the door of the cave
  So the pretender could never rise from the grave:
And we spread the news in our writing and talking
  That the body's resurrection was only a myth.

Our life was governed by the Stalin of reason;
  Reason divorced from the person, understanding
    from the man;
At that time we didn't hear the heart's old reasons
  Or the spirit's voice: man was not two, but one.

When the atom was split, our materialism was split,
  The old marriage of mind and flesh was discovered:
Man was not one, but three – body, soul and spirit;
  The old, poor, restless, needy Trinity.

Flesh quarrelling with spirit, spirit arguing with flesh
  Within the narrow circle of self's arrogance:
And in the crisis the Spirit was heard opening the
    Scripture
  To sinners travelling on the road to Emmaus.

Our foundations were so unstable; our certainty was
    so rotten;
  So shaky in a court, for it was impudently unfair
To set our evidence against the evidence of those who
    were there,
  The testimony of the eleven's eyes and ears.

After our defeat in the court the Spirit helped us
  Gradually to move the stone from the grave:
And we smelt Mary's perfumes there, and saw the
    emptiness
  And the cloths and napkin set out so tidy and neat.

(Gwreiddiau, 1959)

30. Pantycelyn

You travelled through the land, heaven's troubadour,
With the Holy Spirit's degree in your wallet,
You were the chief poet of His Eisteddfod
The licensed teacher of all the little rhymesters:
You saw your King on His stallion, His sword
Reaping the battles of the world, the flesh and the devil,
And in His Palace you drank His wine, His cider and
    His mead,
And wove his eulogy and praise.
You sang to countrymen, chained to the earth
Like oxen all their lives,
In their own dialect, the song of faith
You heard on the branchless tree of the Cross,
And raised them above bog and rock and steep
And set them at the round tables of God's finest food.

(*Ysgubau'r Awen*, 1939)

Notes

Pantycelyn William Williams of Pantycelyn (1717–91), the Carmarthenshire hymnwriter and poet. Pantycelyn spent much of his life on horseback, travelling around Wales to give spiritual guidance and leadership to the newly founded Methodist *seiadau* (meetings at which people would discuss their spiritual experiences). He would take a supply of booklets of his latest hymns with him in his saddlebags and sell them on his journeys.

troubadour Gwenallt uses the word *clerwr*. In the strictly regulated order of Welsh bards the *clerwr* came bottom of the list. He was a travelling rhymester who was not allowed to visit the homes of the gentry, but had instead to depend on the patronage of the poorer sections of society. Pantycelyn did not use the traditional metres of Welsh poetry and therefore would be regarded by professional and classical Welsh poets as a mere *clerwr*.

the Holy Spirit's degree In the bardic order poets would become the pupils of more experienced and qualified poets. They would be awarded a certificate or licence that would permit them to visit the homes of the gentry and enable them to receive gifts as a reward for their poems. Pantycelyn's only poetic qualification is the degree awarded to him by the Holy Spirit.

the chief poet of His Eisteddfod The *pencerdd* (literally 'chief of song') was at the opposite end of the bardic hierarchy to the *clerwr*. He was the greatest of all and acclaimed as such after competing with his fellow poets at an Eisteddfod. In the modern National Eisteddfod of Wales two poets are honoured. The *coron* (crown) goes to the winner of the free metre poetry competition. The *cadair* (chair), the greatest prize of all, goes to the victor in a competition for the best traditional strict metre poem. Although Pantycelyn was a *clerwr* in the eyes of the poetic establishment, in the Eisteddfod of the Spirit he was the *pencerdd*.

licensed teacher of all the little rhymesters Despite his lack of official poetic status, the Holy Spirit licensed Pantycelyn to become the teacher and pattern for other Welsh hymnwriters.

You saw your King on His stallion Medieval Welsh court poets traditionally praised the martial achievements of their princes. One of Pantycelyn's most famous verses begins '*Marchog, Iesu, yn llwyddiannus, gwisg dy gleddau yng ngwasg dy glun*' ('Ride on, Jesus, successfully, wear your sword against your thigh').

In their own dialect Pantycelyn is sometimes criticized by Welsh literary purists for his frequent use of colloquialisms and Carmarthenshire dialect.

31. Saunders Lewis

For Wales's sake you were a fool,
A fool like all of Christ and Mary's martyrs,
They threw their stupid balls at you
Like some Aunt Sally on a fairground booth:
You were thrown away amongst England's rubbish,
One of her crime birds on a lonely perch,
And Welshmen, behind your back, with their
    treacherous hands
Putting bile on top of the grey wormwood.
You were not wounded; it didn't affect you,
Because Wales built a fortress around you,
Whose polished stones their devilishness and power
Can never penetrate,
And the Virgin Mary stands, like a tower above,
Extinguishing each fireball with her holy mantle.

(*Ysgubau'r Awen*, 1939)

Notes

Saunders Lewis (1893–1985), a dramatist, novelist, poet and literary
critic, was one of the founders of Plaid Cymru. In 1936 Lewis, the
writer D. J. Williams and the Baptist minister Lewis Valentine gave
themselves up to the police after symbolically setting fire to building
materials for the intended RAF bombing school at Penyberth in
the Welsh-speaking heartland of the Llŷn Peninsula. After a jury in
Caernarfon failed to convict the three men the trial was transferred
to London. Lewis, Williams and Valentine were sentenced to nine
months' imprisonment, which they served in Wormwood Scrubs.
Swansea University dismissed Saunders Lewis from his post as lecturer in the Welsh Department.

the Virgin Mary stands Saunders Lewis converted to Roman Catholicism in 1932. His father was a Calvinistic Methodist minister.

32. The Nuns

You came like distant doves into our sky
From the cells of Ystrad Fflur and Glyn-y-Groes,
And threw yourselves like those who've lost their way
Into the feeble forest of our stormy age:
You don't stop on the roof, on guttering or joists,
Or linger on our streets amongst the crowd,
No one sees Christ's rings on your feet
Or reads the messages beneath your feathers.
When the storm ebbs and the wind dies down
And the sap comes to the trunk and the leaves to the
   branches,
You'll rise up from the forest as before
With ash and oak leaves in your beaks,
And stand above on the roof of heaven's halls
And the leaves will make His heart rejoice.

(*Ysgubau'r Awen*, 1939)

Note

Ystrad Fflur and Glyn-y-Groes Ystrad Fflur (Strata Florida) was a
Cistercian abbey in mid-Cardiganshire. It was responsible for
founding a convent at Llanllŷr. Glyn-y-Groes (Valle Crucis) was a
Cistercian abbey in north-east Wales.

33. Sin

When we strip off every kind of dress,
The cloak of respectability and wise knowledge,
The cloth of culture and the silks of learning;
The soul's so bare, so uncleanly naked:
The primitive mud is in our poor matter,
The beast's slime in our marrow and our blood,
The bow's arrow is between our finger and thumb
And the savage dance is in our feet.
As we wander through the original, free forest,
We find between the branches a piece of Heaven,
Where the saints sing anthems of grace and faith,
The *Magnificat* of His salvation;
We raise our nostrils up like wolves
Baying for the Blood that redeemed us.

(*Ysgubau'r Awen*, 1939)

34. The Churches

They are old ships behind the floodgates,
  Lurking in the mud and the sludge;
Rust on their anchors, dirt on their bows,
  Their decks unpainted and their sails in rags:
They lean as if they've got arthritis
  In their limbs, and can't get up:
They've forgotten about the sea except when the
    floodgate lets
  A hint of the tide flow in to them.

They've been cast aside by the industrial
  And scientific flood of our world:
The passion of rebirth isn't behind their sails,
  Only a thin and cosy religiousness.
The Queen and the regiments' flags are on their
    masts,
  And the Captain forbids beer and wine:
Chattering about the Sabbath and religious systems
  Forgetting man's ecumenical suicide.

If they asked the Breath to lift the floodgates
  And ventured out into the irrational sea;
Their anchor greased, their sails confident,
  And faith on deck and window and door:
They would see the Christ who was technologically
    nailed
  To His plutonium Cross;
Getting down from it; taming the waters
  And choking the nuclear storms of our age.

(*Gwreiddiau*, 1959)

35. Astray

A pity we know the words without knowing the
    Word
And sell our souls for the fair's confetti and toffee,
Following every drum, dancing after every flute
Drowning Intercession's hymn with the rhyme of the
    Absolute.

Men in South Wales without a drink or food or a fag,
And the pride of their district under heaps of scrap,
    cinders and slag:
The canal stagnant in villages, without shout or
    movement or sound
And the pot-bellied rats ripping up the bodies of dogs
    and cats.

The gods who walk our lands are fortune and fate
    and chance,
And we are like moles who've been caught in their
    trap;
There's neither devil nor hell under our world's paper
    floors,
Heaven's candles have been snuffed and the angels all
    strangled.

The generation's mouth contains dust, and chest's pus
    in its spit,
A she-wolf in the wilderness bays for the moon's daft
    whoring:
The barbarians' halls are packed out, church and altar
    are widowed,
Our ship loiters in the mist, crew and captain are
    plastered.

O Mary, set Your Star in the midst of heaven's
   darkness,
And show with your chart the path back to His will,
Come down between tangled ropes, put your hand on
   the helm,
And guide our obstinate ship to one of God's ports.

(Ysgubau'r Awen, 1939)

Notes and References

Donald Allchin: Discovering a New World

1. Robert Rhys, 'Poetry 1939–1970', in Dafydd Johnston (ed.), *A Guide to Welsh Literature, Circa 1900–1990* (Cardiff, 1998), pp. 91–2. In Welsh the same word is used both for dove and for pigeon.
2. This poem is quoted and discussed in Chapter Four of A. M. Allchin, *Resurrection's Children, Exploring the Way Towards God* (Norwich, 1998).
3. Dyfnallt Morgan, *The Oxford Book of Welsh Verse in English* (Oxford, 1977), pp. 200–201.
4. Peter Lord, 'Insider Artists and Industrial Society', *The Visual Culture of Wales: Industrial Society* (Cardiff, 1998), pp. 174–222.
5. Ibid., p. 183.
6. Ibid., pp. 191–2.
7. Ibid, p. 197. Peter Lord uses this picture for the front cover of his book.
8. Tony Conran, *Welsh Verse, Translations* (3rd edn., Bridgend, 1992), p. 93.
9. Idris Foster, 'Review of Y Coed', *Poetry Wales*, Vol. 5, No. 3 (Spring 1970), p. 53.
10. The Welsh version is in J. E. Meredith, *Gwenallt, Bardd Grefyddol* (Llandysul, 1974), pp. 55–79, and the English version is in *Planet*, 32 (June 1976) pp. 1–10.
11. A. M. Allchin, *Praise Above All: Discovering the Welsh Tradition* (Cardiff, 1991), p. 140.
12. Donald Nicholl, *Triumphs of the Spirit in Russia* (London, 1997), p. 190.
13. Helen Gardener, *The Composition of Four Quartets* (Oxford, 1978), p. 118.
14. T. S. Eliot, *The Complete Poems and Plays* (London, 1969), p. 197.

15. Ibid., p. 281.
16. Ibid., p. 192.
17. Ibid., p. 197.
18. Vladimir Lossky, *Sept Jours sur les Routes de France Juin 1940* (Paris, 1998), p. 61.
19. Ibid., p. 52.
20. Ibid., p. 53.
21. David Jones, *The Dying Gaul and Other Writings* (London, 1978), pp. 38–9.
22. Bobi Jones, *Crist a Chenedlaetholdeb* (Llandysul, 1994), p. 86.
23. Ibid., pp. 86–7.
24. Quoted by Helen Gardener, *The Composition of Four Quartets*, pp. 210–11.
25. Waltraut J. H. Stein, 'Reflections on Edith Stein's Secret', in *Spiritual Life, A Quarterly of Contemporary Spirituality*, Vol. 34, No. 3 (1988), p. 134. The writer is a great-niece of Edith Stein.
26. Waldo Williams, *The Peacemakers*, trans. Tony Conran (Llandysul, 1998), p. 175.

D. Densil Morgan: Gwenallt: Poet of Flesh and Spirit

1. C. S. Lewis, *Surprised by Joy* (London, 1972), pp. 182–3.
2. *Credaf: Llyfr o Dystiolaeth Gristionogol*, ed. J. E. Meredith (Aberystwyth, 1943), p. 64; a translation of Gwenallt's essay entitled 'What I Believe' was published in *Planet* 32 (1976), pp. 1–10.
3. *Credaf*, pp. 59, 61.
4. H. A. Hodges, 'Gwenallt', *Sobornost* 6 (1970), p. 29.
5. M. Wynn Thomas' deconstructionalist reading of 'The Dead' is to be found in John Rowlands (ed.), *Sglefrio Ar Eiriau* (Llandysul, 1992), pp. 15–20, while Robert Rhys' critique is contained in R. Rhys (ed.), *Patrwm Amryliw*, (Barddas, 1997), pp. 155–64 and in Dafydd Johnston (ed.), *A Guide to Welsh Literature, c. 1900–1996* (Cardiff, 1998), pp. 90–5.
6. See e.g. John Rowlands 'Ein duwiol brydyddion', *Y Weiren Bigog* 1 (1985), 'Atgyfodi dadl', *Taliesin* 64 (1988), pp. 80–88 and *Cnoi Cil ar Lenyddiaeth* (Llandysul, 1989), pp. 70–78.
7. See D. Densil Morgan, *The Span of the Cross: Christian Religion and Society in Wales 1914–2000* (Cardiff, 1999), pp. 181–219.
8. *Poetry Wales* 6 (1970), p. 54. For a lucid exposition of this poem, in English, see Alun Page, 'Valiant for Truth: some comments on the elegy "John Edward Daniel" by Gwenallt', *The Anglo-Welsh Review* 19 (1970), pp. 32–43.
9. Ned Thomas, *The Welsh Extremist* (London, 1971), p. 42.

Key Dates in the Life of
D. Gwenallt Jones

1899   Gwenallt (David James Jones) born May 18th at
           Wesley Terrace, Pontardawe, Glamorgan.
1910   Goes to the county school in Ystalyfera.
1917–19   In prison as a conscientious objector.
1919   Commences as a student at University College
           Aberystwyth.
1921   Wins the Chair in the Student Eisteddfod, for his
           poem *Ynys Enlli* (Bardsey Island).
1925   School teacher in Barry, Glamorgan.
1926   Wins the Chair at the National Eisteddfod, Swansea,
           for his poem *Y Mynach* (The Monk).
1927   Becomes lecturer in the Welsh department of
           University College Aberystwyth.
1931   Wins the Chair at the National Eisteddfod Bangor.
1937   Marries Nell Edwards at Aber-arth, Ceridigion; one
           daughter, Mair.
1943   Essay on his beliefs in *Credaf* (I Believe), ed. J. E.
           Meredith.
1944   Confirmed by the Bishop of St David's; worships at
           parish church of Llanbadarn Fawr.
1957   Returns to the Presbyterian Church and becomes a
           member of Tabernacle Chapel, Aberystwyth.
1961   Visits Israel.
1961–5   Editor of the quarterly periodical *Taliesin*.
1967   Honorary Doctorate of Letters from the University of
           Wales.
1968   Dies at Aberystwyth on Christmas Eve.

Gwenallt: Further Reading

Here are some descriptions and critiques of Gwenallt's work in English.

H. A. Hodges, 'Gwenallt: an English view of the poet', *Planet* 29 (1975), pp. 24–9

Dafydd Johnston, *A Guide to the Literature of Wales* (University of Wales Press, Cardiff, 1994), pp. 99–101

Robin Chapman and Robert Rhys in Dafydd Johnston (ed.), *A Guide to Welsh Literature*, circa 1900–1990 (University of Wales Press, Cardiff, 1998), pp. 79–85, 89–95

Gwyn Jones and John Rowlands, *Profiles: A Guide to Writing in Twentieth Century Wales* (Gomer, Llandysul, 1980), pp. 70–5

Dyfnallt Morgan, *D. Gwenallt Jones* (University of Wales Press, Cardiff, 1972)

Dafydd Rowlands, *Bro a Bywyd Gwenallt* (a photographic account of his life and work) (Welsh Arts Council, Cardiff, 1982)

Meic Stephens (ed.), *The New Companion to the Literature of Wales* (University of Wales Press, Cardiff, 1972), pp. 371–3

Ned Thomas, *The Welsh Extremist: a Culture in Crisis* (Victor Gollancz, London, 1971), pp. 40–51; 3rd edition published as *The Welsh Extremist: Modern Welsh Politics, Literature and Society* (Lolfa, Talybont, 1991), pp. 45–57

The publication of this book coincides with the last stages of the preparation of a complete edition of Gwenallt's poems in the original: Christine James (ed.), *Cerddi Gwenallt: Y Casgliad Cyflawn* (Gomer, Llandysul, 2000)